Lecture Notes in Computer Science 10381

Commenced Publication in 1973
Founding and Former Series Editors:
Gerhard Goos, Juris Hartmanis, and Jan van Leeuwen

More information about this series at http://www.springer.com/series/7407

Alessandro Abate · Sylvie Boldo (Eds.)

Numerical Software Verification

10th International Workshop, NSV 2017
Heidelberg, Germany, July 22–23, 2017
Proceedings

 Springer

Editors
Alessandro Abate (iD)
University of Oxford
Oxford
UK

Sylvie Boldo
Université Paris-Sud, Inria
Orsay
France

j

ISSN 0302-9743   ISSN 1611-3349   (electronic)
Lecture Notes in Computer Science
ISBN 978-3-319-63500-2   ISBN 978-3-319-63501-9   (eBook)
DOI 10.1007/978-3-319-63501-9

Library of Congress Control Number: 2017932122

LNCS Sublibrary: SL1 – Theoretical Computer Science and General Issues

Printed on acid-free paper

This Springer imprint is published by Springer Nature
The registered company is Springer International Publishing AG
The registered company address is: Gewerbestrasse 11, 6330 Cham, Switzerland

Preface

The 10th International Workshop on Numerical Software Verification (NSV 2017) was held during July 22–23, 2017, in Heidelberg, Germany.

This year NSV 2017 took place alongside the International Workshop on Formal Methods for Rigorous Systems Engineering of Cyber-Physical Systems (RISE4CPS, a one-time, invite-only event, chaired by Ezio Bartocci of TU Vienna). NSV 2017 was co-located within CAV 2017, the 29th International Conference on Computer-Aided Verification.

The scope of NSV 2017 has broadened since the earlier editions, but its core retains known fundamental aspects. Numerical computations are ubiquitous in digital systems: Monitoring, supervision, prediction, simulation, and signal processing rely heavily on numerical calculus to achieve desired goals. Design and verification of numerical algorithms has a unique set of challenges, which set it apart from the rest of software verification. To achieve the verification and validation of global system properties, numerical techniques need to precisely represent the local behaviors of each component. The implementation of numerical techniques on modern hardware adds another layer of approximation because of the use of finite representations of infinite precision numbers that usually lack basic arithmetic properties, such as associativity. Finally, the development and analysis of cyber-physical systems (CPS), which involve interacting continuous and discrete components, pose a further challenge. It is hence imperative to develop logical and mathematical techniques for reasoning about programmability and reliability. The NSV workshop is dedicated to the development of such techniques.

NSV 2017 was a two-day event, featuring two invited talks, single-track regular podium sessions, and additionally four invited speakers providing tutorials within RISE4CPS.

In all, 18 Program Committee members helped to provide at least four reviews of the submitted contributions, which were presented during the single-track sessions and appear as full papers in these proceedings.

A highlight of NSV 2017 was the presence of two high-profile invited speakers: Kyoko Makino, Professor in the Department of Physics and Astronomy at Michigan State University (USA), gave a seminar titled "Verified Computations using Taylor Models and the Applications." Nathalie Revol, researcher at Inria (Lyon, France), gave a talk titled "Introduction to the IEEE 1788-2015 Standard for Interval Arithmetic."

Further details on NSV 2017 are featured on the website: http://www.cs.ox.ac.uk/conferences/NSV17/

Finally, a few words of acknowledgment are due. Thanks to Springer for publishing the NSV proceedings in its *Lecture Notes in Computer Science* series. Thanks to Sergiy Bogomolov and Pavithra Prabhakar from the Steering Committee for support, to Yassamine Seladji for the help with publicity, to Viraj Wijesuriya for the organization of the workshop website, to all the Program Committee members and additional reviewers for their work in ensuring the quality of the contributions to NSV 2017, and to all the participants for contributing to this event.

June 2017   Alessandro Abate
                                                                        Sylvie Boldo

Organization

Program Committee Chairs

Alessandro Abate	University of Oxford, UK
Sylvie Boldo	Inria, France

Program Committee

Stanley Bak	Air Force Research Lab - Information Directorate, USA
Sergiy Bogomolov	IST Austria
Olivier Bouissou	The Mathworks, USA
Martin Brain	University of Oxford, UK
Alexandre Chapoutot	ENSTA ParisTech, France
Pieter Collins	Maastricht University, The Netherlands
Lucas Cordeiro	University of Oxford, UK
Eva Darulova	Max Planck Institute for Software Systems, Germany
Georgios Fainekos	Arizona State University, USA
François Févotte	EDF, France
Susmit Jha	SRI International, USA
James Kapinski	Toyota, USA
Guillaume Melquiond	Inria, France
Ian Mitchell	University of British Columbia, Canada
Sylvie Putot	LIX, Ecole Polytechnique, France
Sriram Sankaranarayanan	University of Colorado, USA
Walid Taha	Halmstad University, Sweden/Rice University, USA
Alexander Wittig	ESA ESTEC, Netherlands

Steering Committee

Sergiy Bogomolov	Australian National University, Australia
Radu Grosu	TU Vienna, Austria
Matthieu Martel	Université de Perpignan, France
Pavithra Prabhakar	Kansas State University, USA
Sriram Sankaranarayanan	University of Colorado, USA

Additional Reviewer

Franck Vedrine

Keynote Abstracts

Verified Computations Using Taylor Models and Their Applications

Kyoko Makino and Martin Berz

Michigan State University, East Lansing, MI 48824, USA
{Makino,berz}@msu.edu
http://bt.pa.msu.edu

Abstract. Numerical methods assuring confidence involve the treatment of entire sets instead of mere point evaluations. We briefly review the method of interval arithmetic that is long known for rigorous, verified computations, and all operations are conducted on intervals instead of numbers. However, interval computations suffer from overestimation, the dependency problem, the dimensionality curse, and the wrapping effect, to name a few, and those difficulties often make conventional interval based verified computational methods useless for practical challenging problems.

The method of Taylor models combines Taylor polynomials and remainder error enclosures, and operations are now conducted on Taylor models, where the bulk amount of the functional dependency is carried in the polynomial part, and the error enclosures provides a safety net to rigorously guarantee the result. Using simple and yet challenging benchmark problems, we demonstrate how the method works to bring those conventional difficulties under control. In the process, we also illustrate some ideas that lead to several Taylor model based algorithms and applications.

Introduction to the IEEE 1788–2015 Standard for Interval Arithmetic

Nathalie Revol

Inria – LIP, ENS de Lyon, University of Lyon
46 allée d'Italie, 69364 Lyon Cedex 07, France

Nathalie.Revol@inria.fr

Abstract. Interval arithmetic is a tool of choice for numerical software verification, as every result computed using this arithmetic is self-verified: every result is an interval that is guaranteed to contain the exact numerical values, regardless of uncertainty or roundoff errors.

From 2008 to 2015, interval arithmetic underwent a standardization effort, resulting in the IEEE 1788–2015 standard. The main features of this standard are developed: the structure into levels, from the mathematic model to the implementation on computers; the possibility to accommodate different mathematical models, called flavors; the decoration system that keeps track of relevant events during the course of a calculation; the exact dot product for point (as opposed to interval) vectors.

Keynote Abstracts for RISE4CPS

CounterExample Guided Synthesis of Sound Controllers for Cyber-Physical Systems with SAT Solvers

Alessandro Abate

Department of Computer Science, University of Oxford, Oxford, UK
aabate@cs.ox.ac.uk

We consider a classical model setup for Cyber-Physical Systems, comprising a physical plant represented as a linear, time-invariant model, which is closed loop with a digitally-implemented controller. As a key CPS feature, the plant model is given as a dynamical equation with inputs, evolving over a continuous state space, whereas the control signals are discrete in time and value.

The goal is to design a controller with a linear architecture ensuring that the closed-loop plant is safe, and at the same time accounting for errors due to the signals digitalisation, the manipulation of quantities represented with finite word length, and finally possible imprecisions in the description of the plant model.

We present a sound and automated approach based on counterexample guided inductive synthesis (CEGIS). The CEGIS architecture encompasses two phases: a synthesis step and a verification phase. We first synthesise a feedback controller that stabilises the plant but that may not be safe; safety is thereafter verified either via BMC or abstract acceleration. If the verification step fails, a counterexample is provided to the synthesis engine and the process iterates.

We demonstrate the practical value of this new CEGIS-based approach by automatically synthesising digital controllers for numerous models of physical plants extracted from the control literature. The details of this work appear in [2], which generalises work in [1]: the latter characterises models by transfer functions and exclusively considers stabilisation objectives.

References

1. Abate, A., Bessa, I., Cattaruzza, D., Cordeiro, L., David, C., Kesseli, P., Kroening, D.: Sound and automated synthesis of digital stabilizing controllers for continuous plants. In: HSCC 2017, pp. 197–206 (2017)
2. Abate, A., Bessa, I., Cattaruzza, D., Cordeiro, L., David, C., Kesseli, P., Polgreen, E., Kroening, D.: Automated formal synthesis of digital controllers for state-space physical plants. In: CAV 2017 (2017, to Appear)

Supported in part by the Alan Turing Institute, London, UK. Joint work at the University of Oxford with Iury Bessa, Dario Cattaruzza, Lucas Cordeiro, Cristina David, Pascal Kesseli, Daniel Kroening, and Elizabeth Polgreen.

Techniques and Tools for Hybrid Systems Reachability Analysis

Erika Ábrahám

RWTH Aachen University, Aachen, Germany

Hybrid systems are systems with combined discrete and continuous behaviour, typical examples being physical systems controlled by discrete controllers. Such systems can be found in various fields such as aviation, control engineering, medicine, or the wide field of cyber-physical systems.

The increasing relevance of hybrid systems, especially systems which interact with humans, requires careful design and proper *safety verification* techniques. Whereas the verification of purely continuous or purely discrete systems are already well-established research areas, the combination of discrete and continuous behaviours brings additional challenges for formal methods.

Logical formalisations are used in theorem-proving-based tools like KEYMAERA [12], ARIADNE [4], or the ISABELLE/HOL-based tool described in [10]. Other tools like DREACH [11], ISAT-ODE [6] and HSOLVER [13] also use logical characterisations but in combination with interval arithmetic and SMT solving. The tool C2E2 [5] uses validated numerical simulation; Bernstein expansion is implemented in [15]. This variety is complemented by approximation methods like hybridization, linearisation and abstraction techniques to increase the applicability of hybrid systems verification.

In this tutorial we focus on *flowpipe-construction-based* techniques and their implementation. As the reachability problem for hybrid systems is in general undecidable, flowpipe-construction-based reachability analysis techniques usually compute *over-approximations* of the set of reachable states of hybrid systems: starting from some initial sets, their time trajectories (*flowpipes*) and successors along discrete transitions (*jump successors*) are over-approximated in an iterative manner. Some tools in this area are CORA [1], FLOW* [3], HYCREATE [9], HYSON [2], SOAPBOX [8], and SPACEEX [7].

The development of such tools is effortful, as datatypes for the underlying state set representations need to be implemented first. Our free and open-source C++ library HYPRO [14] provides implementations for the most prominent state set representations, with the aim to offer assistance for the rapid implementation of new algorithms by encapsulating all representation-related issues and allowing the developers to focus on higher-level algorithmic aspects.

In this tutorial we give an introduction to hybrid systems, and to flowpipe-construction-based algorithms for computing their reachable state sets. After discussing theoretical aspects, we shortly describe available tools and introduce in more

This work was supported by the German Research Council (DFG) in the context of the HyPro project.

detail our HʏPʀᴏ library, explain its functionalities, and give some examples to demonstrate its usage.

References

1. Althoff, M., Dolan, J.M.: Online verification of automated road vehicles using reachability analysis. IEEE Trans. Robot. **30**(4), 903–918 (2014)
2. Bouissou, O., Chapoutot, A., Mimram, S.: Computing flowpipe of nonlinear hybrid systems with numerical methods. CoRR abs/1306.2305 (2013). http://arxiv.org/abs/1306.2305
3. Chen, X., Ábrahám, E., Sankaranarayanan, S.: Flow*: An analyzer for non-linear hybrid systems. In: Sharygina, N., Veith, H. (eds.) CAV 2013. LNCS, vol. 8044, pp. 258–263. Springer, Berlin (2013)
4. Collins, P., Bresolin, D., Geretti, L., Villa, T.: Computing the evolution of hybrid systems using rigorous function calculus. In: ADHS 2012, pp. 284–290. IFAC-PapersOnLine (2012)
5. Duggirala, P., Mitra, S., Viswanathan, M., Potok, M.: C2E2: A verification tool for Stateflow models. In: Baier, C., Tinelli, C. (eds.) TACAS 2015. LNCS, vol. 9035, pp. 68–82. Springer, Berlin (2015)
6. Eggers, A.: Direct handling of ordinary differential equations in constraint-solving-based analysis of hybrid systems. Ph.D. thesis, Universität Oldenburg, Germany (2014)
7. Frehse, G., et al.: SpaceEx: acalable verification of hybrid systems. In: Gopalakrishnan, G., Qadeer, S. (eds.) CAV 2011. LNCS, vol. 6806, pp. 379–395. Springer, Berlin (2011)
8. Hagemann, W., Möhlmann, E., Rakow, A.: Verifying a PI controller using SoapBox and Stabhyli: Experiences on establishing properties for a steering controller. In: ARCH 2014. EPiC Series in Computer Science, vol. 34. EasyChair (2014)
9. HyCreate: A tool for overapproximating reachability of hybrid automata. http://stanleybak.com/projects/hycreate/hycreate.html
10. Immler, F.: Tool presentation: Isabelle/hol for reachability analysis of continuous systems. In: ARCH14-15. EPiC Series in Computer Science, vol. 34, pp. 180–187. EasyChair (2015)
11. Kong, S., Gao, S., Chen, W., Clarke, E.M.: dReach: δ-reachability analysis for hybrid systems. In: Baier, C., Tinelli, C. (eds.) TACAS 2015. LNCS, vol. 9035, pp. 200–205. Springer, Berlin (2015)
12. Platzer, A., Quesel, J.: KeYmaera: A hybrid theorem prover for hybrid systems (system description). In: Armando, A., Baumgartner, P., Dowek, G. (eds.) IJCAR 2008. LNCS, vol. 5195, pp. 171–178. Springer, Berlin (2008)
13. Ratschan, S., She, Z.: Safety verification of hybrid systems by constraint propagation based abstraction refinement. In: Morari, M., Thiele, L. (eds.) HSCC 2005. LNCS, vol. 3414, pp. 573–589. Springer, Berlin (2005)
14. Schupp, S., Ábrahám, E., Ben Makhlouf, I., Kowalewski, S.: HyPro: A C++ library for state set representations for hybrid systems reachability analysis. In: Barrett, C., Davies, M., Kahsai, T. (eds.) NFM 2017. LNCS, vol. 10227, pp. 288–294. Springer, Cham (2017)
15. Testylier, R., Dang, T.: NLTOOLBOX: a library for reachability computation of nonlinear dynamical systems. In: Van Hung, D., Ogawa, M. (eds.) ATVA 2013. LNCS, vol. 8172, pp. 469–473. Springer, Cham (2013)

ProbReach: Probabilistic Bounded Reachability for Uncertain Hybrid Systems

Fedor Shmarov and Paolo Zuliani

School of Computing Science, Newcastle University, Newcastle upon Tyne, UK
{f.shmarov,paolo.zuliani}@ncl.ac.uk

Abstract. We give an overview of our recent work on verified probabilistic reachability for hybrid systems with uncertain parameters [1–3]. Essentially, the problem reduces to computing validated enclosures for reachability probabilities. We present two approaches: one has high computational cost and provides absolute guarantees on the correctness of the answers, *i.e.*, the computed enclosures are formally guaranteed to contain the reachability probabilities. The other approach combines rigorous and statistical reasoning, thereby yielding better scalability by trading absolute guarantees with statistical guarantees. We exemplify both approaches with case studies from systems biology and cyber-physical systems.

The tutorial is divided into three parts:

1. introduction to delta-satisfiability and delta-complete decision procedures;
2. probabilistic bounded delta-reachability;
3. ProbReach tool demo.

No previous knowledge of systems biology or cyber-physical systems is necessary.

References

1. Shmarov, F., Zuliani P.: ProbReach: verified probabilistic δ-reachability for stochastic hybrid systems. In: HSCC, pp. 134–139. ACM (2015)
2. Shmarov, F., Zuliani, P.: Probabilistic hybrid systems verification via SMT and Monte Carlo techniques. In: Bloem, R., Arbel, E. (eds.) HVC 2016. LNCS, vol. 10028, pp. 152–168. Springer, Cham (2016)
3. Shmarov, F., Zuliani, P.: SMT-based reasoning for uncertain hybrid domains. In: AAAI-16 Workhop on Planning for Hybrid Systems, 30th AAAI Conference on Artificial Intelligence, pp. 624–630 (2016)

Data-Driven Verification of Cyber-Physical Systems with DryVR and C2E2

Sayan Mitra

Department of Electrical and Computer Engineering, Coordinated Science
Laboratory, University of Illinois at Urbana-Champaign, Urbana, IL 61801, USA
mitras@illinois.edu

Abstract. Data-driven verification algorithms combine static analysis of models
of control systems with dynamic information generated from executions or
simulations. For cyber-physical systems and complex control systems,
promising new algorithms and tools have been developed over the past five
years following this approach. These methods have been used in verifying
challenging benchmark problems correctness of air-traffic control protocols,
meta-stability of mixed signal circuits, temporal properties of engine control
systems, and safety related problems arising in autonomous vehicles and
advanced driving assist systems. In this tutorial, I will give an overview of two
verification tools that embody recent developments in data-driven verification,
namely C2E2 and DryVR. Both use simulation or execution data; while C2E2
relies on static analysis of detailed dynamic models and give deterministic
guarantees, DryVR only uses black-box simulators and gives probabilistic
guarantees. Thus, the latter can check systems with partially known models. We
will discuss some of the recent case studies and open problems in the area.

Contents

Keynote Abstracts

Verified Computations Using Taylor Models and Their Applications

Kyoko Makino$^{(\boxtimes)}$ and Martin Berz

Michigan State University, East Lansing, MI 48824, USA
{makino,berz}@msu.edu
http://bt.pa.msu.edu

Abstract. Numerical methods assuring confidence involve the treatment of entire sets instead of mere point evaluations. We briefly review the method of interval arithmetic that is long known for rigorous, verified computations, and all operations are conducted on intervals instead of numbers. However, interval computations suffer from overestimation, the dependency problem, the dimensionality curse, and the wrapping effect, to name a few, and those difficulties often make conventional interval based verified computational methods useless for practical challenging problems.

The method of Taylor models combines Taylor polynomials and remainder error enclosures, and operations are now conducted on Taylor models, where the bulk amount of the functional dependency is carried in the polynomial part, and the error enclosures provides a safety net to rigorously guarantee the result. Using simple and yet challenging benchmark problems, we demonstrate how the method works to bring those conventional difficulties under control. In the process, we also illustrate some ideas that lead to several Taylor model based algorithms and applications.

Keywords: Taylor model · Interval arithmetic · Verified computation · Reliable computation · Range bounding · Function enclosure · Verified global optimization · Verified ODE integration

1 Interval Arithmetic

Numerical methods assuring confidence involve the treatment of entire sets instead of mere point evaluations. The method of interval arithmetic (see, for example, [1–3] and many others) is a long known method to support such rigorous, verified computations. Instead of numbers, all operations are conducted on intervals. Furthermore, floating point inaccuracies are accounted for by rounding lower bounds down and upper bounds up. Here are some basic operations of interval arithmetic for intervals $I_1 = [L_1, U_1]$, $I_2 = [L_2, U_2]$.

© Springer International Publishing AG 2017
A. Abate and S. Boldo (Eds.): NSV 2017, LNCS 10381, pp. 3–13, 2017.
DOI: 10.1007/978-3-319-63501-9_1

$$I_1 + I_2 = [L_1 + L_2, U_1 + U_2],$$
$$I_1 - I_2 = [L_1 - U_2, U_1 - L_2],$$
$$I_1 \cdot I_2 = [\min\{L_1 L_2, L_1 U_2, U_1 L_2, U_1 U_2\}, \max\{L_1 L_2, L_1 U_2, U_1 L_2, U_1 U_2\}],$$
$$1/I_1 = [1/U_1, 1/L_1], \quad \text{if } 0 \notin I_1. \tag{1}$$

One can obtain rigorous range bounds of the function by evaluating a function in interval arithmetic.

The basic concept is rather simple, hence the computation is reasonably fast in practice, however interval computations have some severe disadvantages, limiting their applicability for complicated functions. First, the width of resulting intervals scales with the width of the original intervals. Second, artificial blow-up usually occurs in extended calculations. The next trivial example illustrates the blow-up phenomenon dramatically. We compute the subtraction of the interval $I = [L, U]$ from itself, where the width of I is $w(I) = U - L$.

$$I - I = [L, U] - [L, U] = [L - U, U - L],$$
$$w(I - I) = (U - L) - (L - U) = 2(U - L). \tag{2}$$

The resulting width $w(I - I)$ is twice the original width, even though $x - x = 0$. This artificial blow-up is caused by lack of the dependency information. There are various attempts to avoid such a situation like detecting such cancellations ahead of time, but ultimately it is unavoidable in complicated function evaluations. Another practical limitation is the dimensionality curse. As we will see in an example below, practical interval computations require to divide a domain of interest into much smaller sub-intervals, and in the case of multiple dimensions, the computational expense grows very fast. Thus, while providing rigorous estimates, the method suffers from some practical difficulties. The dependency problem leads to overestimations to the extent that in some cases, the estimates may be rigorous but practically useless.

2   A Simple and Yet Challenging Example

To review some range bounding methods, we use a one dimensional function, which is simple enough so that some of the estimates can be performed even by hand calculations. The problem was originally proposed by Moore [4]. Bound the function [5,6]

$$f(x) = 1 + x^5 - x^4 \quad \text{in } [0, 1]. \tag{3}$$

The problem appears to be exceedingly simple, but conventional function range bounding methods on computers find it rather difficult to perform the task near the minimum, which is the reason why Moore was interested in it.

The function profile is shown by solid curve in Fig. 1, and the exact bound B_{exact} can be hand calculated easily, thus the problem serves as an excellent benchmark test for rigorous computation methods. The function takes the maxima at the end points $x = 0$ and $x = 1$, and the minimum at $x = 4/5$.

$$B_{\text{exact}} = \left[f\left(\frac{4}{5}\right), f(0) = f(1) \right] = \left[1 + \left(\frac{4}{5}\right)^5 - \left(\frac{4}{5}\right)^4, 1 \right]$$

$$= \left[1 - \frac{4^4}{5^5}, 1 \right] = [0.91808, 1],$$

$$w(B_{\text{exact}}) = \frac{4^4}{5^5} = 0.08192. \tag{4}$$

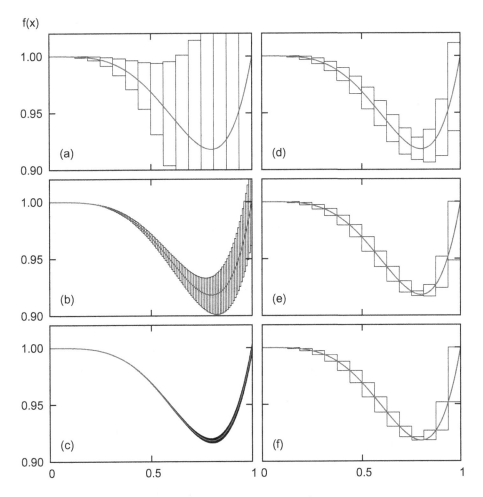

Fig. 1. Range bounding of the function $f(x) = 1 + x^5 - x^4$ in $[0, 1]$ in divided subdomains [5,6]. Using interval arithmetic in (a) 16, (b) 128, (c) 1024 subdomains. Using Taylor models (TM) in 16 subdomains (d) by first order naive TM bounding, (e) by fifth order naive TM bounding, (f) by LDB [6–8] on the fifth order TMs.

We note in passing that the two numerical values in the above estimates happen to be exact as written and are not merely approximations.

To begin the investigation on the function range bounding performance in interval arithmetic, we evaluate the function on the entire domain $[0, 1]$.

$$f([0, 1]) = 1 + [0, 1]^5 - [0, 1]^4 = 1 + [0, 1] - [0, 1] = [0, 2],$$
$$w(f[0, 1]) = 2. \tag{5}$$

The function range bound $f([0, 1])$ certainly encloses the exact bound B_{exact}, but it is uselessly overestimated.

The next step is to divide the entire domain into smaller subdomains. This helps to decrease the overestimation to obtain much sharper function range bound. The entire domain $[0, 1]$ is divided into smaller and smaller equi-sized subdomains, and interval arithmetic is conducted to evaluate the function range bound in each subdomain. Figure 1(a) shows the situation using 16 equi-sized subdomains, and we observe still quite large overestimations around the minimum. The frame size is fixed for all the pictures in Fig. 1 to compare different methods and settings easily. Most of the function sub range bounds are out of the vertical frame size in the case of 16 domain intervals. Much smaller equi-sized subdomains are shown in Fig. 1(b), (c). With 128 equi-sized subdomains (b), the function sub range bounds almost fit in the vertical frame size, however one observes the difficulty near the minimum and the rightward. With 1024 equi-sized subdomains (c), the function sub range bounds get quite sharp. The bound over the entire domain is obtained as the union of all the sub bounds. See the resulting bound estimates in Table 1. Despite the simple appearance of the problem description, indeed the interval method has a hard time to deal with this problem.

3   The Method of Taylor Models

We have been proposing the method of Taylor models, consisting of Taylor expansions and the remainder error enclosures, hence supporting rigorous, verified computations. As we describe below, Taylor models carry richer information, and despite the more complicated structures of the method compared to conventional rigorous numerical methods like interval arithmetic, the method offers an economical means to complicated practical problems.

For a function $f : D \subset R^v \rightarrow R$ that is $(n + 1)$ times continuously partially differentiable, denote the n-th order Taylor polynomial of f around the expansion point $x_0 \in D$ by $P(x - x_0)$, and bound the deviation of P from f by a small remainder bounding set e.

$$f(x) - P(x - x_0) \in e, \quad \forall x \in D \text{ where } x_0 \in D. \tag{6}$$

We call the combination of P and e as a Taylor model.

$$T = (P, e) = P + e. \tag{7}$$

T depends on the order n, the domain D, and the expansion point x_0. For two Taylor models $T_1 = (P_1, e_1)$ and $T_2 = (P_2, e_2)$ with the same conditions n, D, and x_0, we define Taylor model addition and multiplication as follows:

$$T_1 + T_2 = (P_1 + P_2, e_1 + e_2),$$
$$T_1 \cdot T_2 = (P_{1 \cdot 2}, e_{1 \cdot 2}), \tag{8}$$

where $P_{1 \cdot 2}$ is the part of the polynomial $P_1 \cdot P_2$ up to the order n, and the higher order part from $(n+1)$ to $2n$ is kept in $P_{>n}$. Denoting an enclosure bound of P over D by $B(P)$, we have

$$e_{1 \cdot 2} = B(P_{>n}) + B(P_1) \cdot e_2 + B(P_2) \cdot e_1 + e_1 \cdot e_2 \tag{9}$$

where operations on remainder bounding sets e_i follow set theoretical operations and outward rounding in other suitable representative sets.

Using these, intrinsic functions for Taylor models can be defined by performing various manipulations. Refer to [7,9] for the details on definitions of standard intrinsic functions as well as the computer implementations. Obtaining the integral with respect to variable x_i of P is straightforward, so one can obtain an integral of a Taylor model straightforwardly. Thus we have an antiderivation ∂_i^{-1} in Taylor model arithmetic.

The method provides enclosures of any function given by a finite computer code list by an n-th order Taylor polynomial and a remainder error enclosure with a sharpness that scales with order $(n+1)$ of the width of the domain D. It alleviates the dependency problem in the calculation, and it scales favorably to higher dimensional problems.

4   Range Bounding of the Example by Taylor Models

As mentioned, Taylor models can be used for range bounding of functions. Even a crude method of evaluating a bound of P provides good function range bounds compared to conventional range bounding methods in interval arithmetic; evaluate bounds of all the monomials, then sum them up together with the remainder enclosure. Taylor polynomials in the structure of Taylor models allow more sophisticated algorithms such as the Linear Dominated Bounder (LDB) and the Fast Quadratic Bounder (QFB) [6–8].

First, we demonstrate a function evaluation in Taylor model arithmetic by hand calculation. We express the variable x covering the entire domain $[0,1]$ by a Taylor model as

$$x \in T_x = P_x + e_x \quad \text{with} \quad P_x = 0.5 + 0.5 \cdot x_0, \quad e_x = 0, \quad x_0 \in [-1,1]. \tag{10}$$

Before proceeding to the next step, let us examine the self subtraction as in Eq. (2) in the interval case. We subtract the Taylor model T_x from itself.

$$T_x - T_x = (P_x - P_x, e_x - e_x)$$
$$= ((0.5 + 0.5 \cdot x_0) - (0.5 + 0.5 \cdot x_0), 0 - 0) = (0, 0). \tag{11}$$

After performing the necessary cancellation in the polynomial part, the resulting Taylor model is $(0, 0)$. We note that the corresponding calculations of Eqs. (10) and (11) on computers produce nonzero remainder error enclosures by accounting for floating point representation errors associated to the polynomial arithmetic of Taylor models on computers. So, the error enclosure e_x is nonzero even though it is extremely tiny near the floating point accuracy floor, and the error enclosure of $T_x - T_x$ is a few times of e_x, where the part $e_x - e_x$ produces the same effect as seen in Eq. (2), though the size is negligible, i.e., about 10^{-15} in double precision computations.

With T_x prepared in Eq. (10), we now evaluate the function f of Eq. (3) in the fifth order Taylor model arithmetic. This can be done by hand calculation with moderate effort:

$$
\begin{aligned}
T_{f,5} = f(T_x) &= 1 + (T_x)^5 - (T_x)^4 \\
&= 1 + (0.5 + 0.5 \cdot x_0 + 0)^5 - (0.5 + 0.5 \cdot x_0 + 0)^4 \\
&= 1 + 0.5^5 \cdot \left(1 + 5x_0 + 10x_0^2 + 10x_0^3 + 5x_0^4 + x_0^5 + 0\right) \\
&\quad - 0.5^4 \cdot \left(1 + 4x_0 + 6x_0^2 + 4x_0^3 + x_0^4 + 0\right) \\
&= 1 + 0.5^5 \cdot \left(-1 - 3x_0 - 2x_0^2 + 2x_0^3 + 3x_0^4 + x_0^5\right) + 0. \quad (12)
\end{aligned}
$$

The function $f(x)$ is a fifth order polynomial, thus the most accurate Taylor model representation of the function is achieved by a fifth order Taylor model, resulting in a zero remainder error enclosure. When the Taylor model arithmetic computation is performed on computers, a tiny nonzero remainder error enclosure will result. If lower order Taylor models are used, the order of the polynomial is truncated by the order used, and the higher order polynomial contributions are lumped into the remainder error enclosure.

Using $T_{f,5}$ in Eq. (12), we evaluate a function range bound. The simplest way is to sum up the bound contributions from each monomial in the polynomial part of $T_{f,5}$ utilizing $x_0, x_0^3, x_0^5 \in [-1, 1]$ and $x_0^2, x_0^4 \in [0, 1]$. This method is called naive Taylor model bounding.

$$
\begin{aligned}
f_{TM_5} &\in 1 + 0.5^5 \cdot (-1 - 3 \cdot [-1, 1] - 2 \cdot [0, 1] + 2 \cdot [-1, 1] + 3 \cdot [0, 1] + [-1, 1]) \\
&\in 1 + 0.5^5 \cdot [-9, 8] = [0.71875, 1.25], \\
w(f_{TM_5}) &= 0.5^5 \cdot (8 + 9) = 0.53125, \quad (13)
\end{aligned}
$$

where we note that the numerical values happen to be exact as written and not merely approximated. Compared to the interval estimate in Eq. (5), this estimate is much sharper but still much wider than the exact bound B_{exact}.

As a usual procedure, one divides the entire domain into smaller subdomains. We divide the entire domain $[0, 1]$ into 16 equi-sized subdomains, and a function range bound is evaluated in each subdomain by the naive fifth order Taylor model bounding, and the resulting situation is shown in Fig. 1(e). As a reference, we also performed the naive first order Taylor model bounding as shown in Fig. 1(d). The 5th order naive Taylor models bound the function range quite accurately, in fact better than the 1024 divided intervals, but even the first order naive Taylor models with 16 subdomains perform better than the 128 divided intervals.

To further improve the accuracy in Taylor model based computations, it is more efficient and economical to use advanced bounding algorithms than dividing the subdomains further. The behavior of a function is characterized primarily by the linear part, and the accuracy of the linear representation increases as the domain becomes smaller, except when there is a local extremum, in which case the quadratic part becomes the leading representative of the function. Taylor models carry the information on the Taylor expansion to the order n by definition, and this means that there are linear and quadratic, and also higher order terms explicitly as coefficients of the polynomial P, and one does not elaborate to obtain them. This is a significant advantage of the Taylor model method compared to other rigorous methods like the interval method that does not have any automated mechanism to obtain such information.

The Linear Dominated Bounder (LDB) and the Fast Quadratic Bounder (QFB) utilize the linear, and the quadratic part respectively, and both are practically economical methods while providing excellent range bounds [6–8]. In the 16 equi-sized subdomains, we evaluated the fifth order Taylor models of the function as before, and we applied the LDB method for function range bounding. The resulting situation is shown in Fig. 1(f), having very tight range bounding. Table 1 summarizes the bounding performances. Both LDB and QFB are applicable to multivariate functions, and both can be used for multi-dimensional pruning to eliminate the area in the domain which does not contribute to range bounding.

Table 1. Range bounding of the function $f(x) = 1 + x^5 - x^4$ in $[0, 1]$. Unless exact, the bound values are rounded outward. The GO method does not use equi-sized subdomains, involving pruning and deleting of subdomains.

Method		Division	Lower bound	Upper bound	Width	Ref.
Exact		1	0.91808	1	0.08192	Eq. (4)
TM	GO, 5th	3 (8 steps)	0.918079	1.000001	0.081922	Sect. 4.1
	LDB, 5th	16	0.918015	1.000001	0.081986	Fig. 1(f)
	Naive, 5th	16	0.916588	1.000030	0.083442	Fig. 1(e)
	Naive, 1st	16	0.906340	1.011237	0.104897	Fig. 1(d)
	Naive, 5th	1	0.71875	1.25	0.53125	Eq. (13)
Interval		1024	0.916065	1.003901	0.087836	Fig. 1(c)
		128	0.901137	1.030886	0.129749	Fig. 1(b)
		16	0.724196	1.227524	0.503328	Fig. 1(a)
		1	0	2	2	Eq. (5)

4.1   Verified Global Optimizations Using Taylor Models

We have seen the sharpness and the efficiency of function range bounding tasks when Taylor models are utilized. Using the above discussed methods, we have developed an efficient rigorous, verified global optimization (GO) tool for general purposes, combining all the economically available information of the objective function and the tools in a smart way. In the search domain, which is a multi-dimensional box in general, we apply a branch-and-bound approach, and the reached solution is a guaranteed range bound of the true minimum in the entire search domain. The Taylor model based verified global optimization tool has been successfully applied to challenging optimization problems, starting from benchmark problems such as Eq. (3) to practical optimization problems in chaotic dynamical systems, astrodynamics, and particle accelerators. We refer the reader for the details to, for example, [5,6,8].

The resulting function range bound of the global optimization tool for the problem in Eq. (3) is listed in Table 1, showing that it provides an optimal solution, agreeing with the exact bound B_{exact} up to the floating point representation errors. The division of the domain is not made ahead of time, but a division is done as needed in the branch-and-bound approach. Furthermore, pruning and discarding of subdomains are performed for the purpose of narrowing the search area. In this example, starting from the initial search domain $[0,1]$ as the first step, the optimal solution is reached in 8 branch-and-bound steps, involving 2 bi-secting divisions (thus 3 subdomains), 3 LDB-then-QFB pruning, and 2 QFB-alone pruning.

5   Applications Utilizing Taylor Models

Besides the function range bounding and the verified global optimization methods discussed above, there are various other Taylor model based algorithms possible for obtaining verified solutions, for example, integrations of functions, differential equations, determining inverses, fixed point problems, implicit equations, and some others [9]. Having an antiderivation ∂_i^{-1} in the Taylor model arithmetic is particularly useful to deal with the problems involving integrations. Especially verified ODE integrations using Taylor models have been successfully applied to many benchmark problems and practical problems in chaotic dynamical systems, astrodynamics, and particle accelerators.

5.1   Verified Integrations of ODEs

The various techniques of rigorous integrations using Taylor models have been developed to carry out a long-term integration; see, for example, [7,10–12]. Conventional verified ODE integration methods based on intervals further suffer from the wrapping effect in addition to the standard difficulties such as the dependency problem, the overestimation problem, and the dimensionality curse. When conducting numerical ODE integrations, the solution of the previous time step is carried over to the next time step, where it is treated as the initial condition in the momentary one time step. In verified ODE integrations, the solutions of the time steps as well as the initial conditions are sets with nonzero volume instead of mere points, and the shape of the sets necessarily deforms as the integration evolves. So, even though one starts an integration from a box shaped initial condition set, for which intervals can describe the set perfectly, after one time step, the solution set would not have a boxed shape. Then, the solution set has to be re-packaged into a larger box to include the deformed solution set, and intervals can describe a re-packaged larger box again. Such geometric inflation due to re-packaging is called the wrapping effect. There are various techniques to reduce the wrapping effect, but, one way or another, it cannot be avoided in interval based ODE integrators.

In the framework of Taylor models, an initial condition set is described by Taylor models as in Eq. (10), where the Taylor model T_x expresses the variable x covering a domain. A solution set of a one time step of a Taylor model based ODE integration is again Taylor models; the comparable situation is Eq. (12), where the result of the function evaluation via Taylor model arithmetic is a Taylor model. The solution Taylor models of the one time step are carried over to the next time step as the initial condition Taylor models for the next time step. Other than the treatment of the remainder term enclosures, which are of substantially smaller magnitude, here is no re-packaging necessary, thus no wrapping effect. There are various ways to effectively treat remainder enclosures, see, for example, [12].

To conduct a successful long term verified integration using Taylor models, nevertheless, it is important to control the growth of the remainder error enclosures and the nonlinearity of the solutions, as otherwise the error enclosures eventually grow too large to continue the computation. An analogous idea to the sub-divisions in the function range bounding tasks is to control the time step size and the object size of the solution. A combination of the automatic time step size control and the automatic domain decomposition of Taylor model objects allows more robust and longer time verified ODE integrations.

5.2 The Volterra Equations

We illustrate the performance of the Taylor model based verified integration method using a classical problem in the field of verified ODE integrations. The Volterra equations describes dynamics of two conflicting populations.

$$\frac{dx}{dt} = 2x(1 - y), \quad \frac{dy}{dt} = -y(1 - x). \tag{14}$$

The fixed points are $(0,0)$ and $(1,1)$, and the solutions satisfy the constraint condition

$$C(x,y) = xy^2 e^{-x-2y} = \text{Constant}. \tag{15}$$

In $x, y > 0$, the contour curves of $C(x,y)$ form closed curves, and a solution follows a closed orbit counterclockwise around the fixed point $(1,1)$, where outer orbits take longer to travel one cycle. The nonlinearity combined with the periodicity makes the problem a classical benchmark case for verified ODE solvers [2,11].

We choose the initial condition set as a big square centered at $(1,3)$, and the period of the closed orbit of the center point $(1,3)$ is about 5.488138468035 [11]. We integrate the next big initial condition box

$$(x_i, y_i) \in (1,3) + ([-0.5, 0.5], [-0.5, 0.5]) = ([0.5, 1.5], [2.5, 3.5]) \qquad (16)$$

using various Taylor model based techniques until $T = 5.488$. And the Taylor model solution manifold at $T = 5.488$ is shown in Fig. 2 in solid red curves. The solution manifold consists of 17 Taylor model pieces as a result of the automatic domain decomposition technique. The outer part revolves slower, thus it gradually drags behind, causing the difficulty to verified ODE integrators due to the quickly developing nonlinearity. By controlling the size of the momentary Taylor model solution piece by the automatic domain decomposition, the Taylor model integration can keep integrating forward for a much longer time while producing more Taylor model solution pieces. In Fig. 2, three contour curves are drawn in dashed green, corresponding to the center point and the outermost and the innermost points in the initial condition box, serving as a visual guide for the solution to stay inside. In this example case, the remainder error enclosures of the solution Taylor model pieces stayed below 3×10^{-4}, a size is unrecognizable in the picture.

To put the results into perspective, let us look at some performances in the conventional rigorous ODE integration methods based on the interval method.

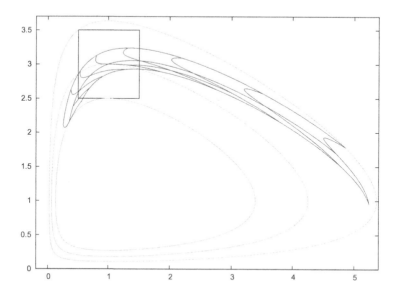

Fig. 2. Taylor model based verified integration of the Volterra equations for the initial condition box $(1,3) \pm 0.5$. The true solution stays inside the guiding contour curves (dashed green). The TM solution at $T = 5.488$ consists of 17 pieces (solid red) as a result of the automatic domain decomposition without noticeable overestimation. (Color figure online)

Earlier in [11], we discussed about Taylor model integration performances for the Volterra equations with the initial condition set centered at the same point $(1, 3)$ but with a much smaller box, namely $(1, 3) + ([-0.05, 0.05], [-0.05, 0.05])$ that is 10×10 times smaller than the problem in Eq. (16). We investigated the performances by AWA [13] that is one of well made and widely spread interval based verified ODE integrators. We started from the much smaller initial condition box, and when starting to turn rightward after going down at left, AWA already started to develop the overestimation. Then, during traveling at the bottom rightward, nonlinearity develops quickly, and the AWA integration broke down around $x = 3.5$ at the bottom at the time around $t = 5$. Despite of various sophisticated techniques utilized in AWA in the limited framework of the interval method, AWA got defeated by the wrapping effect, as the interval based methods cannot represent deformed nonlinear objects well without significant overestimation.

Acknowledgments. For numerous interesting and stimulating discussions, we are thankful to Ramon Moore.

References

1. Moore, R.E.: Interval Analysis. Prentice-Hall, Englewood Cliffs (1966)
2. Moore, R.E.: Methods and Applications of Interval Analysis. SIAM (1979)
3. Alefeld, G., Herzberger, J.: Introduction to Interval Computations. Academic Press, New York, London (1983)
4. Moore, R.E.: Private Communication (2004)
5. Makino, K., Berz, M.: Rigorous global optimization for parameter selection. Vestn. Math. **10**(2), 61–71 (2014)
6. Makino, K., Berz, M.: Range bounding for global optimization with Taylor models. Trans. Comput. **4**(11), 1611–1618 (2005)
7. Makino, K.: Rigorous analysis of nonlinear motion in particle accelerators. Ph.D. thesis, Michigan State University, East Lansing, Michigan, USA. Also MSUCL-1093 (1998)
8. Berz, M., Makino, K., Kim, Y.-K.: Long-term stability of the Tevatron by validated global optimization. Nucl. Instrum. Methods **558**, 1–10 (2006)
9. Makino, K., Berz, M.: Taylor models and other validated functional inclusion methods. Int. J. Pure Appl. Math. **6**(3), 239–316 (2003)
10. Berz, M., Makino, K.: Verified integration of ODEs and flows using differential algebraic methods on high-order Taylor models. Reliable Comput. **4**(4), 361–369 (1998)
11. Makino, K., Berz, M.: Suppression of the wrapping effect by Taylor model-based verified integrators: the single step. Int. J. Pure Appl. Math. **36**(2), 175–197 (2006)
12. Makino, K., Berz, M.: Suppression of the wrapping effect by Taylor model-based verified integrators: long-term stabilization by preconditioning. Int. J. Differ. Equ. Appl. **10**(4), 353–384 (2005)
13. Lohner, R.J.: AWA - software for the computation of guaranteed bounds for solutions of ordinary initial value problems (1994)

Introduction to the IEEE 1788-2015 Standard for Interval Arithmetic

Nathalie Revol$^{(\boxtimes)}$ (iD)

Inria – LIP, ENS de Lyon, University of Lyon,
46 allée d'Italie, 69364 Lyon Cedex 07, France
Nathalie.Revol@inria.fr

Abstract. Interval arithmetic is a tool of choice for numerical software verification, as every result computed using this arithmetic is self-verified: every result is an interval that is guaranteed to contain the exact numerical values, regardless of uncertainty or roundoff errors.

From 2008 to 2015, interval arithmetic underwent a standardization effort, resulting in the IEEE 1788-2015 standard. The main features of this standard are developed: the structure into levels, from the mathematic model to the implementation on computers; the possibility to accommodate different mathematical models, called flavors; the decoration system that keeps track of relevant events during the course of a calculation; the exact dot product for point (as opposed to interval) vectors.

Keywords: Interval arithmetic · Standardization · IEEE 1788-2015

1 Introduction

Interval arithmetic is a valuable tool to perform self-validated numerical computations. Indeed, every calculation is performed using intervals as inputs, which are assumed to enclose the exact value of the considered inputs, and it returns intervals as outputs, which are guaranteed to enclose the exact value of the corresponding outputs. This is the most precious feature of interval arithmetic and it is called the *Fundamental Theorem of Interval Arithmetic*, abbreviated in *FTIA* in the following. It sometimes bears different names, depending on the authors. Let us quote here some big names in interval arithmetic, at least some who published their work in English: Hansen and Walster [3], Moore [10,11], Moore again, with Kearfott and Cloud [12], Neumaier [14], Rump [17], Tucker [19] to cite only a few, in alphabetical order.

Other precious features are best exemplified on Newton's method for the determination of the zeros of a function f on a given interval. First, the use of interval arithmetic permits an effective application of Brouwer theorem: when the new iterate, by Newton's method, is included in the previous one, then this iterate contains a zero for f. Second, the use of an ad-hoc definition of the division makes it possible to separate zeros: in such a case, one iteration of

© Springer International Publishing AG 2017
A. Abate and S. Boldo (Eds.): NSV 2017, LNCS 10381, pp. 14–21, 2017.
DOI: 10.1007/978-3-319-63501-9_2

Newton's method produces two disjoint intervals and it is guaranteed that no zero for f lies in the gap between these two intervals. Quite often, each of these two disjoint new iterates contains a (strict) subset of the zeros.

The community of users of interval arithmetic was willing to preserve these precious features. However, libraries implementing interval arithmetic and interval methods usually laid on different variations on interval arithmetic, on different definitions. Examples are on the one hand the `filib++` library [9], rather close to the set-based flavor, and on the other hand the MPFI library [16], closer to the IEEE 754-2008 standard for floating-point arithmetic [6]. It was thus not possible to build a common basis of programs, test cases and benchmarks. It was then collectively decided upon standardizing interval arithmetic, in order to share the possibilities offered by interval arithmetic. The standardization effort was led under the auspices of IEEE, from October 2008 to July 2015. The bulk of the work was done via e-mail. The standardization effort proceeded via so-called "Motions", or proposals that constituted steps forward. Each motion underwent 3 weeks of discussion and possible amendments, followed by 3 weeks of vote. John Pryce, technical editor, created what is now the text of the standard, using the results of the votes as raw material. The content of the standard is developed now.

2   The Big Picture: Structuration into Levels

It was decided to start from the mathematical level, to have a clear and clean basis, and then to investigate and specify how the mathematical notions translate to the implementation levels. The structuration into levels is borrowed from the IEEE 754-2008 Standard for Floating-Point Arithmetic [6].

The first level is the *mathematical level*: it specifies what an interval on real numbers is, what operations on intervals do and so on.

Level 2 deals with the *discretization* of Level 1 intervals, so that they can be implemented on a computer: it defines

– *interval datums*, that are the representations of entities of Level 1;
– *interval types*, that are finite sets of interval datums.

The issues handled at that level are related to the fact that a continuous world is implemented using a discrete and finite environment.

"*Level 3 is about representation of interval datums – usually but not necessarily in terms of floating-point values*" [7]. The concern here is about the representation of an interval datum, e.g., by its endpoints, and the type of the numeric values used for this representation.

Level 4 is about the *encoding* of these representations. It is really the equivalent of Level 4 for floating-point arithmetic. However, as numerical values are not the subject of this standard, very few in IEEE 1788–2015 is said about Level 4.

The figure summarizes the structuration in levels, the content of each level and the relation between levels. Each topic is detailed below.

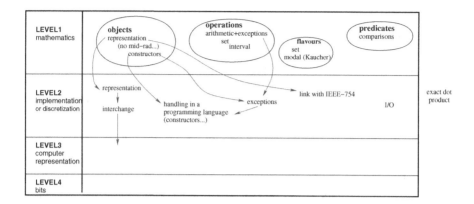

3   Flavors

As it has already been noted, the starting point of this work was a sound definition of interval arithmetic at the mathematical level. Everybody agrees on the meaning of $[1,2] + [3,5]$ but unfortunately no more on the meaning of $[1, +\infty)$, $[4,6]/[0,1]$ or $[2,1]$. Each of these intervals or expressions has a meaning in a specific mathematical model: set theory, Kaucher arithmetic, cset theory, modal arithmetic... but not in all of them, or not the same.

A first choice in the standard is thus to separate what has a common definition in every model, without controversy, from the rest. The standard is designed to accommodate smoothly different models, called *flavors* in the standard, as long as they coincide on common definitions. The standard can thus be seen as a common part and as providing "hooks" where different mathematical models can find a place.

3.1   Common Intervals and Operations

The common definitions and requirements are given in Clause 9 of the standard, entitled "*Operations and related items defined in all flavors*". But first, let us give the definition of a common interval: "The common intervals are defined to be the set $\mathbb{IR}$ of nonempty closed bounded real intervals." [7, Clause 7.2]. Common arithmetic operations include, if x and y denote common intervals: $-x$, $x + y$, $x - y$, xy, x/y if y does not contain 0, x^2, $\sqrt{x}$ if $x \geq 0$, exponential, logarithmic and trigonometric functions on their domain, and a few more.

Two other common operations (even if they sound less than common to you) are cancellative addition and subtraction, that are the reciprocal of addition and subtraction respectively. If $x = [\underline{x}, \bar{x}]$ and $y = [\underline{y}, \bar{y}]$ are two common intervals such that $\bar{x} - \underline{x} \geq \bar{y} - \underline{y}$, then $\mathtt{cancelMinus}(x, y)$ returns the unique interval z such that $y + z = x$, with formula $z = [\underline{x} - \underline{y}, \bar{x} - \bar{y}]$. The operation $\mathtt{cancelPlus}$ is equivalent to $\mathtt{cancelMinus}(x, -y)$.

The set operations of intersection and convex hull of the union of two intervals are also common operations, as well as some operations specific to intervals, such as the left endpoint or the width of an interval.

3.2 Set-Based Flavor and Other Ones

Regarding flavors, it happens that, after many discussions regarding several mathematical models, the only fully developed flavor, and thus the only flavor included in the current version of the standard, is the flavor based on set theory; it is called the *set-based flavor*.

The set-based flavor is described in details in the second part of the standard, Clauses 10 to 14. For brevity, let us simply say that, on top of common intervals, the empty set and unbounded intervals, such as $[1, +\infty)$ are allowed, but not $[2, 1]$. Operations and functions on intervals are defined, in the set-based flavor, as follows: if f is a function and $\boldsymbol{x}_1, \ldots \boldsymbol{x}_n$ are intervals, $f(\boldsymbol{x}_1, \ldots \boldsymbol{x}_n)$ is defined as

$$f(\boldsymbol{x}_1, \ldots \boldsymbol{x}_n) = \mathrm{Hull}\{f(x_1, \ldots x_n) \ : \ x_i \in \boldsymbol{x}_i \text{ for } 1 \leq i \leq n \text{ and } f(x_1, \ldots x_n) \text{ is defined}\}$$

where Hull defines the convex hull of the given set, so as to return an interval. This means that for instance $\sqrt{[-1, 4]} = [0, 2]$ and $\sqrt{[-2, -1]} = \emptyset$. The first example is not a common one as the input interval is not included in the domain of the square root: the result has been computed by intersecting the input interval with the domain of the square root, prior to computing the square root. The second example is not a common one as the result is not a common interval.

In the same way as `cancelMinus` is the reverse operation of the subtraction, several *reverse* functions act on the usual functions; these reverse functions are listed in the standard as mandatory functions. They are highly useful for constraint solving methods. Furthermore, as it permits the use of unbounded intervals, the set-based flavor defines the reverse of the multiplication. This `mulRevToPair` operation is the key element, mentioned in the introduction, to separate zeros in Newton's method.

Other flavors could be added to the IEEE 1788-2015 standard. Flavors that have been considered during the discussions of the working group are Kaucher arithmetic [5], modal arithmetic [1,2] or Rump's proposal to handle the discretization of real intervals [18]. However, the effort has not been pursued until the adoption of the corresponding flavor for the current version of the standard. Anyone willing to propose a new flavor should submit it as a revision of the standard.

4 Decorations

The main requirements for any flavor are, on the one hand, its compatibility with the common part and, on the other hand, the presence of a version of the FTIA. This ensures that the most precious feature of interval arithmetic is preserved.

The last precious feature mentioned in the introduction was that Brouwer theorem is made effective in interval computations. However, an example in the set-based flavor illustrates that a naive use can be misleading. Let us consider the function

$$f \ : \ x \mapsto \sqrt{x} - 1.$$

In $\mathbb{R}$, f has no fixed-point. The evaluation of f over the interval $\boldsymbol{x} = [-1, 4]$ in the set-based flavor yields

$$f(\boldsymbol{x}) = f([-1, 4]) = \sqrt{[-1, 4]} - 1 = [0, 2] - 1 = [-1, 1].$$

This new interval $f(\boldsymbol{x})$ is enclosed in $\boldsymbol{x}$. However Brouwer theorem does not apply in this case, as f is not continuous on $\boldsymbol{x}$ and not even everywhere defined.

The dilemma faced by the working group was thus to choose between two possibilities. The first one consists in returning an invalid value for $f(\boldsymbol{x})$, similar to computations with NaN values in the IEEE 754-2008 standard for floating-point arithmetic, at the risk of getting this invalid value so often that interval arithmetic would be impracticable. The second one consists in returning $f(\boldsymbol{x}) = [-1, 1]$ in this example and in providing the user with a means to check whether the computation encountered "out-of-domain" values during its course. The choice made in the IEEE 1788-2015 standard is the second one: each result comes with a piece of information about the circumstances of its computation.

Furthermore, it has been decided to avoid any kind of global information and to attach this piece of information to the result itself. In the IEEE 1788-2015 standard, this piece of information is called a *decoration* and an interval with a decoration attached to it is a *decorated interval*.

This choice is the result of long and hot discussions within the working group: issues about memory usage (a decoration uses extra memory, perturbs padding...), computation time (each operation must compute its result, but also compute and propagate its decoration) as well as development time (operations get more delicate to implement) were raised.

For common intervals, the only decoration is `common`, abbreviated as `com`. For the set-based flavor, the set of decorations is the set {`com`, `dac`, `def`, `trv`, `ill`}. Here is the meaning of each decoration (what follows is an excerpt of the standard).

Value	Short description	Property	Definition
com	Common	$p_{\text{com}}(f, \boldsymbol{x})$	$\boldsymbol{x}$ is a bounded, nonempty subset of $\text{Dom}(f)$; f is continuous at each point of $\boldsymbol{x}$; and the computed interval $f(\boldsymbol{x})$ is bounded
dac	Defined & continuous	$p_{\text{dac}}(f, x)$	$\boldsymbol{x}$ is a nonempty subset of $\text{Dom}(f)$, and the restriction of f to $\boldsymbol{x}$ is continuous
def	Defined	$p_{\text{def}}(f, \boldsymbol{x})$	$\boldsymbol{x}$ is a nonempty subset of $\text{Dom}(f)$;
trv	Trivial	$p_{\text{trv}}(f, \boldsymbol{x})$	Always true (so gives no information)
ill	Ill-formed	$p_{\text{ill}}(f, \boldsymbol{x})$	Not an Interval; formally $\text{Dom}(f) = \emptyset$

These are listed according to the propagation order, which may also be thought of as a quality-order of $(f, \boldsymbol{x})$ pairs—decorations above `trv` are "good" and those below are "bad".

5   Level 2: Discretization Issues

It has been mentioned that the starting point for every decision in the standard was the mathematical level, or Level 1. Going from Level 1 to Level 2 implies to consider issues related to the use of a finite set of intervals, called an interval type.

Let us assume that the result of some computation, at Level 1, is an interval z. At Level 2, a result must be returned, that belongs to the given interval type and that satisfies the FTIA, i.e., the result must be a representable interval that encloses z. This result can be much larger than z, in case of an overflow: in this case, a bounded interval (at Level 1) can be represented as an unbounded interval at Level 2.

However, the standard prevents an implementation to be too lazy and to return too large intervals. Indeed, it requires that the interval computed at Level 2 is of good quality, by specifying the accuracy of the results: for most operations, the result at Level 2 must be the tightest possible, that is, it is the smallest, for inclusion, interval of the given interval type that encloses z.

Another issue when going from Level 1 to Level 2 is that, at Level 2, every operation must return a result. However, at Level 1, for some operations and some particular inputs, there might be no valid result. When the Level 1 result does not exist, the operation at Level 2 returns either a special value indicating this event (e.g., NaN for most of the numeric functions) or a value considered reasonable in practice. For instance, *the mid() function at Level 2 in the set-based flavor, returns the midpoint of $\emptyset$ as NaN, and of $\mathbb{R}$ as 0; this illustrates flavor-defined values. Both values are undefined at Level 1. It was considered that no numeric value of mid($\emptyset$) makes sense, but that some algorithms are simplified by returning a default value 0 for mid($\mathbb{R}$).*

The relation between a Level 1 operation and a version of it at Level 2, is summarized as follows in the standard. The latter evaluates the Level 1 operation on the Level 1 values denoted by its inputs. If (at those inputs) the operation has no value, an exception is signaled, or some default value returned, or both, in a flavor-defined way. Otherwise the returned value is converted to a Level 2 result of an appropriate Level 2 datatype. If the result is of interval type, overflow may occur in some flavors, causing an exception to be signaled.

Furthermore, implementors of IEEE-1788 compliant libraries raised the following issue: one of the most difficult part in the development of the libraries happened to be the implementation of tight conversions, for instance when the endpoints of an interval have different types. The standard accounts for this difficulty in the following way. *An implementation may support an extended form of literals, e.g., using number literals in the syntax of the host language of the implementation. It may restrict the support of literals at Level 2, by relaxing conversion accuracy of hard cases: rational number literals, long strings, etc. What extensions and restrictions of this kind are permitted is flavor-defined.*

6 Exact Dot Product

Another topic, related to Level 2 exclusively, is the recommendation that the dot product of vectors with scalar, floating-point endpoints, is evaluated as if in exact arithmetic – hence the name of *Exact Dot Product* – up to the final rounding. In particular, no intermediate underflow or overflow is possible. This recommendation is based on the argument that interval arithmetic offers the possibility to get high-quality numerical results. Including the exact dot product in the standard augments the numerical quality of computed results.

7 Libraries Implementing the Standard

Up to the author's knowledge, only two libraries are compliant with the IEEE 1788-2015 standard. One of them, `libieee1788` [13], has been developed by Marco Nehmeier. It is a C++ library that offers every possibility described in the standard. In particular, intervals can be given to constructors with almost any type for each of the endpoints. The other, a bit earlier, library is Octave Interval [4], developed by Oliver Heimlich. As its name suggests, it is called through Gnu Octave, which makes it very easy to use and thus allows to test and check ideas and algorithms very rapidly. To keep the development simple, the only numerical type allowed for the endpoints in particular is the `binary64` (double-precision) format for floating-point numbers defined in [6].

Unfortunately, neither author is still in academy and it is not clear how these libraries will be maintained over time.

8 Conclusion

This succinct summary of the IEEE 1788-2015 standard aims at giving a glimpse of the discussions that led to the development of this standard. The focus was on the less-than-obvious choices that have been made. As implementations, and even more crucially applications, are still in their infancy, no definitive conclusion can be drawn regarding the validity of these choices. The author hopes that this standard will reveal useful for a large audience, through the already available libraries, and wishes that these libraries will find a sustainable support.

Acknowledgments. The author would like to thank Alessandro Abate and Sylvie Boldo for their kind invitation. The author would also like to thank all participants to the working group that developed the IEEE 1788-2015 standard for providing the material for this standard, for their differing points of view that questioned every proposal and that eventually contributed to create a solid standard, and for their never-fading enthusiasm. Last but not least, special thanks go to Kearfott [8] and Pryce [15] for the collective work and for their inspiring papers.

References

1. Goldsztejn, A.: Modal intervals revisited, part 1: a generalized interval natural extension. Reliable Comput. **16**, 130–183 (2012)
2. Goldsztejn, A.: Modal intervals revisited, part 2: a generalized interval mean value extension. Reliable Comput. **16**, 184–209 (2012)
3. Hansen, E.R., Walster, G.W.: Global Optimization Using Interval Analysis, 2nd edn. Marcel Dekker, New York (2003)
4. Heimlich, O.: Interval arithmetic in GNU Octave. In: SWIM 2016: Summer Workshop on Interval Methods (2016)
5. Kaucher, E.: Interval analysis in the extended interval space IR. In: Alefeld, G., Grigorieff, R.D. (eds.) Fundamentals of Numerical Computation (Computer-Oriented Numerical Analysis), pp. 33–49. Springer, Cham (1980). doi:10.1007/978-3-7091-8577-3_3
6. IEEE: Institute of Electrical and Electronic Engineers. 754-2008 - IEEE Standard for Floating-Point Arithmetic. IEEE Computer Society (2008)
7. IEEE: Institute of Electrical and Electronic Engineers. 1788-2015 - IEEE Standard for Interval Arithmetic. IEEE Computer Society, New York, June 2015
8. Kearfott, R.B.: An overview of the upcoming IEEE P-1788 working group document: standard for interval arithmetic. In: IFSA/NAFIPS, pp. 460–465 (2013)
9. Lerch, M., Tischler, G., von Gudenberg, J.W., Hofschuster, W., Krämer, W.: FILIB++ a fast interval library supporting containment computations. Trans. Math. Softw. **32**(2), 299–324 (2006)
10. Moore, R.E.: Interval Analysis. Prentice Hall, Englewood Cliffs (1966)
11. Moore, R.E.: Methods and Applications of Interval Analysis. SIAM Studies in Applied Mathematics (1979)
12. Moore, R.E., Kearfott, R.B., Cloud, M.J.: Introduction to Interval Analysis. SIAM (2009)
13. Nehmeier, M.: libieeep1788: a C++ implementation of the IEEE interval standard P1788. In: 2014 IEEE Conference on Norbert Wiener in the 21st Century (21CW), pp. 1–6. IEEE (2014)
14. Neumaier, A.: Interval Methods for Systems of Equations. Cambridge University Press, Cambridge (1990)
15. Pryce, J.: The forthcoming IEEE standard 1788 for interval arithmetic. In: Nehmeier, M., Wolff von Gudenberg, J., Tucker, W. (eds.) SCAN 2015. LNCS, vol. 9553, pp. 23–39. Springer, Cham (2016). doi:10.1007/978-3-319-31769-4_3
16. Revol, N., Rouillier, F.: Motivations for an arbitrary precision interval arithmetic and the MPFI library. Reliable Comput. **11**(4), 275–290 (2005)
17. Rump, S.M.: Verification methods: rigorous results using floating-point arithmetic. Acta Numer. **19**, 287–449 (2010)
18. Rump, S.M.: Interval arithmetic over finitely many endpoints. BIT Numer. Math. **52**(4), 1059–1075 (2012)
19. Tucker, W.: Validated Numerics - A Short Introduction to Rigorous Computations. Princeton University Press, Princeton (2011)

Precise Numerics

Formal Correctness of Comparison Algorithms Between Binary64 and Decimal64 Floating-Point Numbers

Arthur Blot[1]([✉]), Jean-Michel Muller[1], and Laurent Théry[2]

[1] École Normale Supérieure de Lyon, Lyon, France
arthur.blot@ens-lyon.org, jean-michel.muller@ens-lyon.fr
[2] Inria Sophia Antipolis - Université Côte d'Azur, Sophia Antipolis, France
Laurent.Thery@inria.fr

Abstract. We present a full COQ formalisation of the correctness of some comparison algorithms between binary64 and decimal64 floating-point numbers, using computation intensive proofs and a continued fractions library built for this formalisation.

1 Introduction

Both binary and decimal formats are defined in the IEEE 754-2008 standard. However, no operation is defined to compare them, and the "naïve" approach of converting a decimal floating point number to the closest binary one before comparing it to another binary FP number can lead to inconsistencies. Let us take for example these two FP numbers:

$$x := 7205759403792794/2^{56} \quad \text{(in binary64 format)} \quad > 1/10$$
$$y := 1/10 \quad\quad\quad\quad\quad\quad\quad \text{(in decimal64 format)}$$

If we convert y to the binary64 format, we get x. This means the naïve approach would give that $x \le y$, but actually $x > y$.

The paper [4] by Brisebarre et al. details and proves the correctness of several algorithms which can compare these numbers in a both efficient and entirely reliable way. The initial problem being simple, it would be nice if the algorithms and their correctness proofs were elementary too. This is unfortunately not the case. In particular, the correctness of some of the algorithms requires some non-trivial computation that cannot be performed by hand. The contribution of this paper is to propose a formalisation that carefully checks all the aspects of the correctness proofs.

We use the COQ proof assistant [9] for our formalisation. The paper is organised as follows. In a first section we detail the formal setting in which we have made our formalisation. Then, we present the algorithms and their proof of correctness.

This work was partially funded by the ANR project *FastRelax* (ANR-14-CE25-0018-01) of the French National Agency for Research.

A. Abate and S. Boldo (Eds.): NSV 2017, LNCS 10381, pp. 25–37, 2017.
DOI: 10.1007/978-3-319-63501-9_3

2   Formal Setting

COQ is a generic system that lets us define new objects and build formal proofs of their properties. We are using the FLOCQ library [2] to reason about floating point numbers. These numbers are parametrised by a radix β. They are defined as a record that contains two fields.

```
Record float (beta : radix) := Float { Fnum : Z; Fexp : Z }.
```

For example, the object {|Fnum := 7205759403792794; Fexp := -56|} is a floating-point number whose mantissa is 7205759403792794 and exponent is -56.

In our formalisation, we prove the correctness of the comparison algorithms with respect to the comparison over real numbers. The real numbers are axiomatised in COQ. An abstract type R is defined. A set of properties is assumed that makes it a complete, totally ordered, Archimedean field. On top of this basic field, the standard COQ real library and the COQUELICOT [1] library build the usual real analysis, on top of which the Interval [8] tactic provides us automated proofs of bounds. COQUELICOT contains standard notions like series and limits from which usual functions such as exponential, sine and cosine are defined. Thanks to these libraries, it is possible to give an interpretation of a floating point number as a real number.

```
Definition F2R (f : float beta) := (Fnum f) * beta ^ (Fexp f).
```

The floating point number f represents the real numbers $m \cdot \beta^e$ where m is the mantissa, e the exponent and β the base. Now the problem is simple, we want to build an algorithm eq that takes two floating point numbers f1 and f2 in base 2 and in base 10 respectively and performs an equality test, and an algorithm comp which returns their comparison. Our goal is then to prove that, under some conditions Cond that we will explain later, the following theorem holds:

```
Lemma eq_correct (f1 : float 2) (f2 : float 10) :
  Cond → eq f1 f2 = true ↔ F2R f1 = F2R f2.
```

We use the standard COQ type comparison for the returned type of the comparison function comp. This type contains three elements Lt, Eq, Gt that represent the three possible values of a comparison. The correctness theorem for it looks like:

```
Lemma comp_correct (f1 : float 2) (f2 : float 10) :
  Cond →    comp f1 f2 = Lt ↔ F2R f1 < F2R f2
         ∧ comp f1 f2 = Eq ↔ F2R f1 = F2R f2
         ∧ comp f1 f2 = Gt ↔ F2R f1 > F2R f2.
```

This lemma relates the result of an evaluation of the algorithm comp with a relation between two real numbers.

Note that as real numbers are axiomatised in COQ, we cannot directly compute with them, which makes some proofs more pedestrian and prevents from proving bounds automatically. Fortunately, there exist some tools that address this issue, while keeping the degree of confidence COQ provides. One tool that we are using in this formalisation is the `interval` tactic [8]. It tries to automatically solve goals that contain real expressions by computing an approximation using standard techniques of interval arithmetic. For example, the following error bound of an approximation of the exponential function between 0 and 1 can be proved automatically.

```
Lemma bound_exp_taylor2 x :
  0 ≤ x ≤ 1 → Rabs ((1 + x + x ^ 2 / 2) - exp x) ≤ 22 / 100.
```

Another technique to approximate real numbers are continued fractions. We are using them in our formalisation. Following closely the material that is presented by Khinchin and Eagle [7], we have developed a library to compute and reason about continued fractions inside COQ. Describing the library is outside the scope of this paper. The main basic result that is needed here is that continued fractions represent the best rational approximations one can get. The formal statement is the following.

```
Lemma halton_min (n : nat) (p q : Z) (r : R) :
  0 < q < q[r]_n.+1 → t[r]_n ≤ Rabs (q * r - p).
```

Approximating a real number r by continued fractions can be seen as an iterative process. At rank n, we get an approximation, called convergent, $s_n = p_n/q_n$. One way of quantifying the quality of an approximation p/q is by the value $|qr - p|$. Applied to s_n, this gives $\theta_n = |q_n r - p_n|$, written `t[r]_n` in our formalisation. The previous lemma `halton_min` simply states that the convergent at rank n is the best approximation for all the rational numbers p/q with q less than q_{n+1} (noted `q[r]_n.+1` in the formalisation).

3   Formalisation

Our formalisation contains four algorithms for comparing a binary64 floating-point number and a decimal64 floating-point number and their proof of correctness. The code is available at:

https://gitlab.com/artart78/compbindec

It is composed of five files: `util.v` and `rfrac.v` for general results (most of which are about real numbers or continued fractions), `frac.v` for the result of the continued fraction problem solution, `compformula.v` for the computation of some formulas requiring tabulation of values, and `compbindec.v` for the main result. Altogether, this amounts to about 6500 lines of code that COQ checks in about 25 min. We have been using intensively SSREFLECT [6] for its set of tactics and syntax, the Flocq [2] library for manipulating floating-point numbers, and the Interval [8] tactic for the computation over the real numbers. We had to develop a dedicated library for continued fraction in order to tackle some aspects of the proof. This library is available in the `rfrac.v` file.

We want to compare a binary floating-point number x_2 and a decimal floating-point number x_{10}. This is reflected in our formalisation by introducing two variables of type `float`.

```
Variable x2 : float 2.
Variable x10 : float 10.
```

Furthermore, x_2 belongs to the binary64 format and x_{10} to the decimal64 format. This means that we have:

$$x_2 = M_2 \cdot 2^{e_2 - 52}$$
$$x_{10} = M_{10} \cdot 10^{e_{10} - 15}$$

where:

$$-1022 \leq e_2 \leq +1023 \quad |M_2| \leq 2^{53} - 1$$
$$-383 \leq e_{10} \leq +384 \quad |M_{10}| \leq 10^{16} - 1$$

Without loss of generality, we can also suppose that $x_2 > 0$ and $x_{10} > 0$. If they are of opposite sign, the comparison is trivial (we ignore the differences between $+0$ and -0 in the actual encoding of the numbers) and if they are both negative, taking the opposite of both numbers brings us back to the case we consider.

In our formalisation, as $x_2 > 0$, we normalize it in such a way that we have $2^{52} \leq M_2$. In other terms, we change the exponent and mantissa of subnormal numbers (and widen the bounds of the exponent) so that the mantissa falls into the same bounds as normal numbers. This corresponds to our M2_bound assumption.

```
Definition M2 := Fnum x2.
Hypothesis M2_bound : 2 ^ 52 ≤ M2 ≤ 2 ^ 53 - 1.
Definition e2 := Fexp x2 + 52.
Hypothesis e2_bound : -1074 ≤ e2 ≤ 1023.
```

Similarly for x_{10} but without any shifting, we get

```
Definition M10 := Fnum x10.
Hypothesis M10_bound : 1 ≤ M10 ≤ 10 ^ 16 - 1.
Definition e10 := Fexp x10 + 15.
Hypothesis e10_bound : -383 ≤ e10 ≤ 384.
```

The four hypotheses M2_bound, e2_bound, M10_bound and e10_bound are implicitly conditions of all the theorems we present in the following.

Let us start deriving new facts from these definitions. First, M_{10} can also be "normalized". If we consider $\nu = 53 - \lfloor \log_2(M_{10}) \rfloor$, we have that:

$$0 \leq \nu \leq 53$$

$$2^{53} \leq 2^{\nu} M_{10} \leq 2^{54} - 1$$

These correspond to the theorems v_bound and norm2_bound of our formalisation.

Now, we express x_2 and x_{10} with the largest common power of 2 possible so that both can be expressed as the product of the common power of 2 with a natural number and a power of 2 or 5, respectively. For this, we define $m = M_2$, $n = M_{10}2^\nu$, $h = \nu + e_2 - e_{10} - 37$ and $g = e_{10} - 15$. This gives us the following equalities (theorems x2_eq and x10_eq respectively).

$$x_2 = m \cdot 2^h \cdot 2^{g-\nu} \qquad\qquad x_{10} = n \cdot 5^g \cdot 2^{g-\nu}$$

The initial problem of comparing x_2 and x_{10} reduces to comparing $m \cdot 2^h$ with $n \cdot 5^g$. We also get bounds over m, h, n and g.

$$2^{52} \le m \le 2^{53} - 1$$
$$2^{53} \le n \le 2^{54} - 1$$
$$-398 \le g \le 369$$
$$-1495 \le h \le 1422$$

These are easily proven in CoQ and correspond to the theorems m_bound, n_bound, g_bound and h_bound.

4   Handling "Simple" Cases

The first step of the algorithm consists in checking if the result can be determined by looking at the exponents g and h only. In order to compare 5^g and 2^h, a function φ is introduced. Its definition is the following.

$$\varphi(h) = \lfloor h \cdot \log_5 2 \rfloor$$

It is relatively easy to check that one can determine the result of the comparison between x_2 and x_{10} if g and $\varphi(h)$ differ. Formally, this means that the following two properties hold:

$$\text{If} \quad g < \varphi(h) \quad \text{then} \quad x_2 > x_{10}$$
$$\text{If} \quad g > \varphi(h) \quad \text{then} \quad x_2 < x_{10}$$

They correspond to the theorems easycomp_lt and easycomp_gt in our formalisation.

In order to get an algorithm, one still needs to provide a way to compute $\varphi(h)$. One way to do this is to use the integer value $\lceil 2^k \cdot \log_5 2 \rceil$ for a sufficient large value of k. In our case, $k = 19$ is enough, the following property holds.

$$\varphi(h) = \lfloor h \cdot \lceil 2^{19} \cdot \log_5 2 \rceil \cdot 2^{-19} \rfloor$$

This corresponds to the theorem prop2_1. Unfortunately, such a theorem is outside the reach of the interval tactic which does not handle the floor and to the nearest functions automatically.

In order to overcome this problem, we first use the interval tactic to prove a tight enclosure I of $\log_5 2$. Then, we use the characteristic properties of the rounding functions (x is a real number, y an integer)

$$\lfloor x \rfloor = y \quad \text{iff} \qquad\qquad y \le x < y + 1$$
$$\lceil x \rfloor = y \quad \text{if} \qquad\qquad |x - y| < 1/2$$

For example, in order to prove that $\lceil 2^{19} \cdot \log_5 2 \rceil = 225799$, which is useful to prove the simpler formula $\varphi(h) = \lfloor h \cdot 225799 \cdot 2^{-19} \rfloor$[1]. we reduce the problem to showing that $|2^{19} \cdot \log_5 2 - 225799| < 1/2$ which is solved automatically using the enclosure I. The proof of the prop2_1 theorem is done in a similar way. We first generate the 2918 subgoals that represents all the possible values for h. For each of the subgoals, we guess what the value z for $\lfloor h \cdot \log_5 2 \rfloor$ is. We then need to prove that $\varphi(h) = z$ and $\lfloor h \cdot 225799 \cdot 2^{-19} \rfloor = z$. For both of these goals, we use the characteristic property of the floor function. Showing that $z \leq h \cdot \log_5 2 < z + 1$ and $z \leq h \cdot 225799 \cdot 2^{-19} < z + 1$ is done automatically using the enclosure I. This brute-force method is not the most elegant approach but it works. It takes CoQ 6 min to check the theorem prop2_1.

Once all the properties of the function φ are proved, it is easy to write down an actual algorithm for the simple cases:

```
Definition easycomp : comparison :=
  let h := v + e2 - e10 - 37 in
  let g := e10 - 15 in
  let phih := (225799 * h) / (2 ^ 19) in
  if g < phih then Gt
  else if g > phih then Lt
  else Eq.
```

and derive its associated theorem of correctness:

```
Theorem easycomp_correct:
  (easycomp = Lt → F2R x2 < F2R x10) ∧
  (easycomp = Gt → F2R x2 > F2R x10) ∧
  (easycomp = Eq ↔ g = phi h).
```

Note that we are using the ideal integer arithmetic of CoQ. In a more realistic programming language we would have to deal with bounded arithmetic. Nevertheless, we can run our algorithm on the example given in the introduction and get the expected result.

```
Compute easycomp {| Fnum := 7205759403792794; Fexp := -56 |}
                 {| Fnum :=                  1; Fexp :=  -1 |}.
  = Eq
  : comparison
```

Our correctness theorem tells us that all we can conclude is that $g = \varphi(h)$.

5   Exact Testing

The algorithm in the previous section covers the cases where g differs from $\varphi(h)$. In this section, we assume that $g = \varphi(h)$.

---

[1] Note that this was proved to match the original paper, but all results could have been proven the same way by just using 225799 everywhere instead of $\lceil 2^{19} \cdot \log_5 2 \rceil$.

5.1   Finding the Needed Precision

We define:
$$f(h) = 5^{\varphi(h)} \cdot 2^{-h} = 2^{\lfloor h \log_5 2 \rfloor \cdot \log_2 5 - h}$$

which verifies:

$$f(h) \cdot n > m \Rightarrow x_{10} > x_2$$
$$f(h) \cdot n < m \Rightarrow x_{10} < x_2$$
$$f(h) \cdot n = m \Rightarrow x_{10} = x_2$$

Now, the idea is to get a precise enough approximation of $f(h) \cdot n$ in order to retrieve the exact comparison. Our goal is therefore to find a lower bound η over the smallest non-zero value of the error $|m/n - f(h)|$ in the range where

$$2^{52} \leq m \leq 2^{53} - 1$$
$$2^{53} \leq n \leq 2^{54} - 1$$
$$-787 \leq h \leq 716$$

We can also add an extra constraint that directly comes from the definition of n.

$$\text{If} \quad 10^{16} \leq n \quad \text{then} \quad \text{even}(n)$$

A good candidate for this lower bound, as proposed in [4], is $\eta = 2^{-113.7}$. In order to formally check that this lower bound holds, we split in four the interval of h. For $0 \leq h \leq 53$, it is easy to prove that the lower bound is greater than 2^{-107}. This corresponds to the theorem d_h_easy1. Similarly, the lower bound is greater than 2^{-108} for $-53 \leq h \leq 0$ (d_h_easy2). For the two remaining intervals $54 \leq h \leq 716$ and $-787 \leq h \leq -54$, we make use of our library for continued fractions. The key idea is that in order to find the lower bound for a given h it is not necessary to enumerate all the rationals m/n but only the convergents $s_l = p_l/q_l$ that approximate $f(h)$ and whose denominator are bounded by $2^{53} - 1$. The property that justifies this computation is the following:

$$\text{If} \quad q_l \leq n < q_{l+1} \quad \text{and} \quad |f(h) - m/n| < 1/2n^2 \quad \text{Then} \quad m/n = p_l/q_l$$

This is the conv_2q2 theorem of our library that directly follows the proof given in [7]. In our case, as $\eta = 2^{-113.7}$ and $2^{53} \leq n \leq 2^{54} - 1$, we are sure that $\eta < 1/2n^2$, so our theorem applies.

For the first interval $54 \leq h \leq 716$, the lower bound $\epsilon_p/\epsilon_q \simeq 6.36 \cdot 10^{-35}$ is reached for $h = 612$, $m = 3521275406171921$ and $n = 8870461176410409$. This corresponds to the theorem pos_correct of our formalisation. It is proved by a double enumeration. First, we enumerate all the h from 54 to 716, and for each of them, we enumerate all the convergents of $f(h)$ whose denominator is smaller than $2^{53} - 1$ and check that the error is bigger that ϵ_p/ϵ_q. The entire proof takes 80 s to be checked by CoQ.

For the second interval $-787 \leq h \leq -54$, a similar technique is used. This time the lower bound $\epsilon'_p/\epsilon'_q \simeq 6.05 \cdot 10^{-35}$ is reached for $h = 275$,

$m = 4988915232824583$ and $n = 12364820988483254$. This corresponds to theorem neg_correct and takes $100\,s$ to be validated by CoQ.

The theorem d_h_min collects all the previous results and proves the smallest non-zero error is bigger than $\eta = 2^{-113.7}$. We thus know that if the error is less than η, the distance is 0 and we must be in the equality case.

5.2   Direct Method

The first way to use the previous result is to precompute f in a table indexed by h. Then, assuming μ approximates $f(h) \cdot n$ with accuracy ϵn where $\epsilon < \eta/4$, we have the following implications:

$$
\begin{array}{ll}
\text{If } \mu > m + \epsilon \cdot 2^{54} & \text{Then } \quad x_{10} > x_2 \\
\text{If } \mu < m - \epsilon \cdot 2^{54} & \text{Then } \quad x_{10} < x_2 \\
\text{If } |m - \mu| \le \epsilon \cdot 2^{54} & \text{Then } \quad x_{10} = x_2
\end{array}
$$

where the 2^{54} factor comes from the bound over n.

This corresponds to the theorem direct_method_correct of our formalisation. By computing f we can get an actual algorithm direct_method_alg and its associated correctness theorem direct_method_alg_correct.

Since we have $\eta = 2^{-113.7}$, a 128-bit computed value of f is enough to make the exact comparison. In order to build the algorithm, we first build the table with 1504 entries that contains $\lceil f(h) \cdot 2^{127} \rceil$.

```
Definition f_tbl h : Z :=
  match h with
  | -787 => 15509027532733081403263271342764519407
  | -786 => 77545137663665407016316356713802259704
  | -785 => 38772568831832703508158178356901129852
  ...
  ...
  ...
  |  714 => 75715339914673581502256102241153698026
  |  715 => 37857669957336790751128051120576849013
  |  716 => 94644174893341976877820127801442122533
  | _    => 0
  end.
```

Proving that this table is correct (for each entry i, the value represents $\lceil f(h) \cdot 2^{127} \rceil$) is done by brute force and takes $4\,min$ to be verified. The algorithm then just needs to look up in the table and compare $n \cdot \lceil f(h) \cdot 2^{127} \rceil$ with $m \cdot 2^{127}$.

```
Definition direct_method_alg :=
  let v := n * (f_tbl h) - m * 2 ^ 127 in
  if v < - 2 ^ 57 then Gt
  else if v > 2 ^ 57 then Lt
  else Eq.
```

As we have $2^{124} \leq f(h) \cdot 2^{127} < 2^{128}$, our ϵ is equal to 2^{-124}. This explains the 57 in the algorithm, $57 = -124 + 127 + 54$. The proof of correctness of the algorithm direct_method_alg_correct is a direct consequence of these observations. We have seen in the previous section with the execution of the easycomp algorithm that we have $g = \varphi(h)$ for the example in the introduction. Now, running the direct_method_alg algorithm returns the correct value for the comparison.

```
Compute direct_method_alg
                {| Fnum := 7205759403792794; Fexp := -56 |}
                {| Fnum :=                 1; Fexp :=  -1 |}.
    = Gt
    : comparison
```

The main drawback of this algorithm is that the table may be too large for some realistic implementation. The next section explains how we can alleviate the problem by using a bipartite table.

5.3   Bipartite Table Method

The general idea of this method is that instead of using one single big table, we will use two separate smaller tables and use combination of their values in order to restore all of the information we need.

In this method, we use:

$$q = \lfloor \frac{\varphi(h)}{16} + 1 \rfloor \qquad r = 16q - \varphi(h)$$

such that $f(h) = 5^{16q} \cdot 5^{-r} \cdot 2^{-h}$. We can easily derive the bounds for q and r from the bound of $\varphi(h)$.

$$-21 \leq q \leq 20$$
$$1 \leq r \leq 16$$

In this method, we store 5^{16q} and 5^r after a phase of normalisation. For this, we define the function ψ as follows.

$$\psi(t) = \lfloor t \cdot \log_2 5 \rfloor$$

Similarly to what has been done for $\varphi(h)$, it is easy to compute $\psi(t)$ and $\psi(16q)$ using integer arithmetic:

$$\psi(t) \quad = \lfloor \lfloor 2^{12} \cdot \log_2 5 \rfloor \cdot t \cdot 2^{-12} \rfloor \text{ for } |t| \leq 204$$
$$\psi(16q) = \lfloor \lceil 2^{12} \cdot \log_2 5 \rceil \cdot q \cdot 2^{-8} \rfloor \text{ for } |q| \leq 32$$

These equalities correspond to the theorems prop_2_2 and prop_2_3 in our formalisation. They are proved by brute force in 5 min and 40 s respectively.

Now, we introduce the two functions θ_1 and θ_2 that are defined as follows.

$$\theta_1(q) = 5^{16q} \cdot 2^{-\psi(16q)+127}$$
$$\theta_2(r) = 5^r \cdot 2^{-\psi(r)+63}$$

The following bounds are given by the theorems `theta1_bound` an `theta2_bound`.

$$2^{127} \leq \theta_1(q) < 2^{128} - 1$$
$$2^{63} < \theta_2(r) < 2^{64}$$

Furthermore, we have

$$f(h) = \frac{\theta_1(q)}{\theta_2(r)} 2^{-64-\sigma(h)} \qquad \text{with} \quad \sigma(h) = \psi(r) - \psi(16q) + h$$

If we define Δ as

$$\Delta = \theta_1(q) \cdot n \cdot 2^{-64+8} - \theta_2(r) \cdot m \cdot 2^{8+\sigma(h)}$$

comparing x_2 and x_{10} gives the same result as comparing 0 and Δ (theorem `delta_ineq`). We also easily get that if $x_2 \neq x_{10}$, then $|\Delta| \geq 2^{124}\eta$. This allows us to derive an approximated version of Δ:

$$\tilde{\Delta} = \lfloor \lceil \theta_1(q) \rceil \cdot n \cdot 2^{8-64} \rfloor - \theta_2(r) \cdot m \cdot 2^{8+\sigma(h)}$$

and to prove that comparing 0 with $\tilde{\Delta}$ gives the same result as comparing x_2 with x_{10} (theorem `delta'_ineq`).

```
Definition theta1_tbl q : Z :=          Definition theta2_tbl r : Z :=
match q with                            match r with
 | -21 => 30291069399869299615748576841329007696   | 1 => 11529215046068469760
 | -20 => 33629842688253419175912847062602803678   | 2 => 14411518807585587200
 | -19 => 18668312833510458212900510778566200808   | 3 => 18014398509481984000
 | -18 => 20725990738668607319295523504017132241   | 4 => 11258999068426240000
 | -17 => 23010472126237643618935106442099516590   | 5 => 14073748835532800000
 | -16 => 25546755962044413589201570726871533645   | 6 => 17592186044416000000
 | -15 => 28362596673541699653588533366201411440   | 7 => 10995116277760000000
 ...                                    | 8 => 13743895347200000000
 | 12 => 29833362924800826973163861261851735349    | 9 => 17179869184000000000
 | 13 => 33121686421112380675117871377923490061    | 10 => 10737418240000000000
 | 14 => 18386229439566681806493759420108863345    | 11 => 13421772800000000000
 | 15 => 20412815259847818312725919365334518557    | 12 => 16777216000000000000
 | 16 => 22662777498902795595110325882853306642    | 13 => 10485760000000000000
 | 17 => 25160737381238801985261861341284580098    | 14 => 13107200000000000000
 | 18 => 27934029957198183141977422640250350414    | 15 => 16384000000000000000
 | 19 => 31013003229050298983324099477976554711    | 16 => 10240000000000000000
 | 20 => 17215675123832984696095104991662469280    | _ => 0
 | _ => 0                               end.
end.
```

Fig. 1. Tables for $\lceil \theta_1(q) \rceil$ and $\theta_2(r)$

In order to build the algorithm, we first need to create the two tables for $\lceil \theta_1(q) \rceil$ and $\theta_2(r)$. Our tables are given in Fig. 1. The first one contains integers that fit in 128 bits and the second one in 64 bits. The algorithm first computes q and r, then reads the values of $\lceil \theta_1(q) \rceil$ and $\theta_2(r)$, and then checks the sign of the computed $\tilde{\Delta}$.

```
Definition ineq_alg : comparison :=
  let q := g / 16 + 1 in
  let r := 16 * q - g in
  let psir := (9511 * r) / 2 ^ 12 in
  let psiq := (9511 * q) / 2 ^ 8 in
  let s := psir - psiq + h in
  let a := ((theta1_tbl q) * (n * 2 ^ 8)) / (2 ^ 64) in
  let b := (theta2_tbl r) * (m * 2 ^ (8 + s)) in
  let D := a - b in (0 =?= D)
```

The value 9511 corresponds to $\lceil 2^{12} \cdot \log_2 5 \rceil$ and =?= to the comparison function for integers. We prove the ineq_alg_correct theorem, which is analogous to the other ones. Running the ineq_alg algorithm gives the same value as the one using the direct method.

```
Compute ineq_alg {| Fnum := 7205759403792794; Fexp := -56 |}
                 {| Fnum :=                   1; Fexp :=  -1 |}.
  = Gt
  : comparison
```

6 Equality Case

If we only want to test the equality between x_2 and x_{10}, an even simpler algorithm can be used. We already know that $x_2 = x_{10}$ is equivalent to $m \cdot 2^h = n \cdot 5^g$. As 2 and 5 are relatively prime, only two situations can occur :

- either $5^g \mid m$ and $\quad 2^h \mid n$ with $\quad 0 \le g \le 22$ and $\quad 0 \le h \le 53$;
- or $\quad 2^{-h} \mid m$ and $5^{-g} \mid n$ with $-22 \le g \le 0$ and $-51 \le h \le 0$.

The algorithm is a direct encoding of this property. It checks that $5^g \cdot (n2^{-h}) = m$ if we are in the first case or that $5^{-g} \cdot (m2^h) = n$ if we are in the second case.

```
Definition eq_alg : bool :=
  if (0 ≤ h) && (h ≤ 53) && (0 ≤ g) &&
     (g ≤ 22) && (n mod (2 ^ h) == 0) then
    let m' := 5 ^ g * (n / (2 ^ h)) in m' == m
  else if (h >= -51) && (-22 ≤ g) &&
          (g ≤ 0) && (m mod (2 ^ (-h)) = 0) then
    let n' := 5 ^ (- g) * (m / (2 ^ (- h))) in n' == n
  else
    false.
```

Its correctness theorem proves the equivalence between running the algorithm and testing the two values.

```
Theorem eq_alg_correct : eq_alg = true ↔ (F2R x2 = F2R x10).
```

On our favorite example, it returns the expected result.

```
Compute eq_alg {| Fnum := 7205759403792794; Fexp := -56 |}
               {| Fnum :=                   1; Fexp := -1 |}.
  = false
  : comparison
```

7   Conclusion and Future Works

The main contribution of this work is a careful check of the algorithms and the proofs presented in [4]. In particular, we have connected in a formal way the paper proofs with the computation that is required in order to get the accuracy at which $f(h) \cdot n$ needs to be computed. During the formalisation, we have found some minor mistakes in the original paper and we have also departed at some places from what was presented in the original paper. For example, the original paper states that $-20 \leq q \leq 21$ instead of $-21 \leq q \leq 20$. Fortunately, this mistake has no consequence. More values are tabulated in the actual implementation (the bounds are slightly relaxed). The original paper mentions the bound $2^{-113.67}$ while our formalisation only makes use of $2^{-113.7}$. The statement of the direct_method_correct omits the scaling factor of $f(h)$ in the assumption. It makes its proof easier and simplifies its application. Finally, the statements of the theorems pos_correct and neg_correct do not mention the extra condition (if $h \geq 680$, then $\nu' = h + \varphi(h) - 971 > 0$ and $2^{\nu'} \mid n$) that is present in the original paper. It does not change the lower bound and we believe that this omission makes the statements more readable at the cost of a negligible extra computing.

The capability of computing expressions over the real numbers thanks to the interval tactic has been a key ingredient on this work. These computations are often hidden in the original paper, but detailed in the formal proof. It is the case for example for the bounds for θ_1 and θ_2. The bounds that are obtained without taking into account the bound on h are actually less strict than the ones specified in the paper. For example, only $\theta_1 < 2^{128}$ could be proved, but it is actually important to get the $2^{128} - 1$ bound in order to know we can embed the value into a 128-bit value. The 2^{128} bound was obtained by noticing that $16q \log_2 5 - \lfloor 16q \log_2 5 \rfloor < 1$, but the $2^{128} - 1$ bound requires that it is less than $1 + \log_2(1 - \frac{1}{2^{128}}) \simeq 1 - \frac{1}{2^{128}}$. We successfully managed to formalise all these proofs but clearly life would have been easier if the tactic interval would accommodate the floor and the ceiling functions.

There are several ways to extend this work. First, we could formalise the counting argument that is present in the original paper that quantifies the percentage of floating point numbers that are comparable using the first partial comparison method (easycomp). It would require to develop the notion of cardinal of sets of floating point numbers in the Coq standard library. Second, what we have proven are only algorithms, it would be very interesting to try to prove a realistic software implementation using a tool like Why3 [5]. Finally a sequel of our reference [4] for this work has been written by the same authors in [3]. The general idea of the algorithm remains the same, but the generalisation of the result also requires a generalisation of all the intermediate results, and computation may become a lot harder since the numbers can then take up to 128 bits. Formalising it would be a real challenge.

References

1. Boldo, S., Lelay, C., Melquiond, G.: Coquelicot: a user-friendly library of real analysis for Coq. Math. Comput. Sci. **9**(1), 41–62 (2015)
2. Boldo, S., Melquiond, G.: Flocq: a unified library for proving floating-point algorithms in Coq. In: Antelo, E., Hough, D., Ienne, P. (eds.) 20th IEEE Symposium on Computer Arithmetic, ARITH 2011, Tübingen, Germany, 25–27 July 2011, pp. 243–252. IEEE Computer Society (2011)
3. Brisebarre, N., Lauter, C.Q., Mezzarobba, M., Muller, J.: Comparison between binary and decimal floating-point numbers. IEEE Trans. Comput. **65**(7), 2032–2044 (2016)
4. Brisebarre, N., Mezzarobba, M., Muller, J., Lauter, C.Q.: Comparison between binary64 and decimal64 floating-point numbers. In: Nannarelli, A., Seidel, P., Tang, P.T.P. (eds.) 21st IEEE Symposium on Computer Arithmetic, ARITH 2013, Austin, TX, USA, April 7–10 2013, pp. 145–152. IEEE Computer Society (2013)
5. Filliâtre, J.-C., Paskevich, A.: Why3—where programs meet provers. In: Felleisen, M., Gardner, P. (eds.) ESOP 2013. LNCS, vol. 7792, pp. 125–128. Springer, Heidelberg (2013). doi:10.1007/978-3-642-37036-6_8
6. Gonthier, G., Mahboubi, A.: A small scale reflection extension for the Coq system. Technical report RR-6455, INRIA (2008)
7. Khinchin, A., Eagle, H.: Continued Fractions. Dover Books on Mathematics. Dover Publications, Mineola (1964)
8. Martin-Dorel, É., Melquiond, G.: Proving tight bounds on univariate expressions with elementary functions in Coq. J. Autom. Reason. **57**(3), 187–217 (2016)
9. The Coq Development Team: The Coq Proof Assistant Reference Manual – Version V8.6, December 2016. http://coq.inria.fr

Sound Numerical Computations
in Abstract Acceleration

Dario Cattaruzza[1]($\boxtimes$), Alessandro Abate[1] (iD), Peter Schrammel[2],
and Daniel Kroening[1]

[1] Department of Computer Science, University of Oxford, Oxford, UK
dario.cattaruzza@hotmail.com
[2] School of Engineering and Informatics, University of Sussex, Brighton, UK

Abstract. Soundness is a major objective for verification tools. Methods that use exact arithmetic or symbolic representations are often prohibitively slow and do not scale past small examples. We propose the use of numerical floating-point computations to improve performance combined with an interval analysis to ensure soundness in reach-set computations for numerical dynamical models. Since the interval analysis cannot provide exact answers we reason about over-approximations of the reachable sets that are guaranteed to contain the true solution of the problem. Our theory is implemented in a numerical algorithm for Abstract Acceleration in a tool called Axelerator. Experimental results show a large increase in performance while maintaining soundness of reachability results.

1 Introduction

Linear algebra packages have been developed in various flavours [1,17,23]. While the most formal of these packages use symbolic algorithms to ensure soundness, the most successful tools for large-scale applications sometimes sacrifice numerical soundness in favour of performance [13]. Similar trade-offs can be made in a number of related algorithms. For instance, eigenvalue problems frequently require matrices that are several orders of magnitude larger than those that symbolic evaluation can handle, and thus, are typically solved using floating-point calculations.

Floating-point computations cover a very wide range of problems, and are orders of magnitude faster than both symbolic and rational arithmetic. They are however, subject to rounding errors, which presents a number of challenges [16, 27] that need to be addressed in order to obtain valid results.

The first problem we will focus on is that of soundness. Once an unknown error has been introduced, it is impossible to establish the correctness of the answer (although in most cases it will be correct to a given accuracy, we have no

---

The authors were in part supported by Oxford Instruments PLC, ERC project 280053 (CPROVER), the H2020 FET OPEN 712689 SC^2, and the Alan Turing Institute, London, UK.

© Springer International Publishing AG 2017
A. Abate and S. Boldo (Eds.): NSV 2017, LNCS 10381, pp. 38–60, 2017.
DOI: 10.1007/978-3-319-63501-9_4

way to prove or disprove it). This problem can be solved with the use of interval arithmetic. By rounding outwards (i.e., increasing the size of the interval to include the error), we ensure that the true answer is always contained inside the interval, thus soundness is preserved. Using interval arithmetic can typically increase the computation time by a factor of four (see Sect. 6), which is moderate compared to the speed-up provided by the use of floating points.

The next problem we face regarding rounding errors is that they are cumulative. Each numerical operation performed will typically increase the error by a small amount, leading to a significant error after a large number of operations. When using intervals, this means that although the true result may be contained by the answer, the over-approximation could be large enough as to make this result meaningless. This means that some problems will require higher precision than others (in practice, a multiple precision arithmetic package will allow us to select an arbitrarily large precision). This comes at a cost dependent on the selected precision, so it is important to select an appropriate value for each problem. Algorithms requiring less iterations are therefore preferred to minimise the precision requirements.

The final challenge presented by the use of interval arithmetic appears when using comparisons to make binary decisions. When intervals partially intersect, it may not always be clear what the result of such comparisons should be. Therefore, we need to establish an order for the interval arithmetic.

In the following, we will discuss the above concepts with respect to a representative algorithm that benefits from the use of numerical algorithms. We use Abstract Acceleration [6, 21], which is a method that relies on solving linear programs in their corresponding eigenspaces. Since we look to study large dimensional problems, we work on a convex polyhedral domain, which in the case of 1-dimensional models reduces to standard interval arithmetic.

The main contribution of this work is to develop a sound numerical algorithm for Abstract Acceleration taking care of the errors introduced by the computations at each step. This goal entails the following:

1. We develop a numerical Simplex with error bounds using interval representations that ensures results are sound over-approximations of the original problem, i.e., the true results are always contained in the intervals. We note that, unlike previous work on sound linear solvers, our algorithm can reason about problems with pre-existing bounded errors in the problem statement.
2. We develop a Vertex Enumerator using intervals that ensures that all possible vertices of the original polyhedron (i.e., the expected polyhedron that would be obtained using exact arithmetic) are found within the hypercubes representing each abstracted vertex.
3. We develop a fast algorithm for describing eigenspaces of matrices within known error bounds. While this can largely be achieved using existing packages, the need to integrate multiple precision numbers with interval arithmetic and dealing with Jordan forms while maintaining a reasonable speed has motivated the development of a slightly different implementation.

4. We implement these techniques in the software tool Axelerator.[1]

2 Preliminaries

Our work relies heavily on Interval Arithmetic and Convex Polyhedra, which are defined in the following.

Definition 1. *An interval domain is an abstract domain over the reals that defines a set of numbers by an upper and lower bound. We use the notation:*

$$[x] = [\underline{x}\ \overline{x}] = \{x \in \mathbb{R} \mid \underline{x} \le x \le \overline{x}\} \tag{1}$$
$$]x[=]\underline{x}\ \overline{x}[= \{x \mid \underline{x} < x < \overline{x}\} : x \in \mathbb{R} \tag{2}$$
$$[x[= [\underline{x}\ \overline{x}[= \{x \mid \underline{x} \le x < \overline{x}\} : x \in \mathbb{R} \tag{3}$$

to represent an element of the domain. We also define the operators $+,-,*^{2},/$ *as the sum, subtraction, multiplication and division of an interval, with the following properties:*

$$[x_1] + [x_2] = [(\underline{x}_1 + \underline{x}_2) \quad (\overline{x}_1 + \overline{x}_2)], \tag{4}$$
$$[x_1] - [x_2] = [(\underline{x}_1 - \underline{x}_2) \quad (\overline{x}_1 - \overline{x}_2)], \tag{5}$$
$$[x_1] * [x_2] = [\inf(\underline{x}_1\underline{x}_2, \underline{x}_1\overline{x}_2, \overline{x}_1\underline{x}_2, \overline{x}_1\overline{x}_2) \quad \sup(\underline{x}_1\underline{x}_2, \underline{x}_1\overline{x}_2, \overline{x}_1\underline{x}_2, \overline{x}_1\overline{x}_2)], \tag{6}$$
$$\frac{[x_1]}{[x_2]} = \left[\inf\left(\frac{\underline{x}_1}{\underline{x}_2}, \frac{\underline{x}_1}{\overline{x}_2}, \frac{\overline{x}_1}{\underline{x}_2}, \frac{\overline{x}_1}{\overline{x}_2}\right) \quad \sup\left(\frac{\underline{x}_1}{\underline{x}_2}, \frac{\underline{x}_1}{\overline{x}_2}, \frac{\overline{x}_1}{\underline{x}_2}, \frac{\overline{x}_1}{\overline{x}_2}\right)\right] : 0 \notin [\underline{x}_2\ \overline{x}_2]. \tag{7}$$

Note that division is not defined for denominator intervals containing 0. This case never applies to our algorithms since pivots, which is the only operation requiring division, operate on non-zero values. Additionally, any monotonic function over the reals can be mapped into an interval equivalent as:

$$f(x) \to [f]([x]) = [\inf(f(\underline{x}), f(\overline{x})) \quad \sup(f(\underline{x}), f(\overline{x}))]. \tag{8}$$

In the case of non-monotonic functions, such as trigonometric operations, the calculation of $[f]([x])$ *has to take into consideration the minima and maxima of the function over the interval* $[x]$.

The above definitions are over the reals, which means that the result of any of these operations is exact. However, when using Finite Word Length representations such as floating points, results may not be representable in the given format and are implicitly rounded. In order for interval arithmetic to be sound, these domains must always round the upper limit upwards and the lower limit downwards, thus expanding the interval. These operations are well defined within the IEEE-754 standard [19] as well as in existing multiple precision libraries, such as mpfr [12], so we will not discuss the details here. For a full description of interval arithmetic over IEEE-754 floating point representations see [30].

---

[1] www.cprover.org/LTI.
[2] As standard, we will often omit this operator in the following.

Definition 2. *The support function of a point $x \in \mathbb{R}^n$ in a given direction $v \in \mathbb{R}^n$ is a scalar*

$$\rho_x(v) = x \cdot v, \tag{9}$$

where $\cdot$ is the dot product between vectors. This can be extended to set X, so that $\rho_X(v) = \sup_{x \in X} x \cdot v$.

Definition 3. *A convex polyhedron is an intersection of half-planes in $\mathbb{R}^n$ that is closed and non-empty. It can be described by the equation $Cx \leq d : C \in \mathbb{R}^{m \times n}, x \in \mathbb{R}^n, d \in \mathbb{R}^m$. Each row in C corresponds to a vector normal to a bounding hyperplane of the polyhedron, while the corresponding element in d is the* support function *of the hyperplane. The hyperplane consists of all of the points x that meet the criterion $C_i x = d_i$ (where i denotes the i-th component, and C_i the corresponding row).*

3   Related Work

There are several tools and approaches using numeric computations for reachability analysis of large scale systems. Tools such as FLOW [8] or COSY [31] use Taylor models with remainder errors to calculate reach sets of non-linear systems. Floating point errors are over-approximated by pre-defined metrics on the calculations. SpaceEx [13] uses linear program analysis to rigorously evaluate reach sets. It also offers an option using support functions with numerically unsound calculations to achieve fast results. Similarly, reachability analysis tools relying on numeric algorithms contained in MATLAB [25] are likely to be unsound since error bounds are not typically provided in most of the enclosed algorithms. Set based simulations, like HYSON [3] or HYLAA [2] use set representations such as zonotopes and polyhedra to evaluate reach tubes.

Although a large number of algorithms have been developed to find rigorous bounds for linear equalities [24], there are not as many studies doing the same for optimal solutions over linear inequalities (which is the basis for Polyhedral Analysis). Polyhedral Analysis (as used in [6,13,20]) may require linear decision procedures to find solutions. These procedures would all benefit from numeric implementations with error bounds that meet the requirements for sound over-approximations.

There are historically two decision procedures that are commonly used for linear arithmetic: Fourier-Motzkin elimination and the simplex method. Most SMT solvers implement the latter because of its better performance when using rational arithmetic, while linear abstraction domains favor it for its performance on linear optimization problems. The original simplex has been revised numerous times; in particular, there is a variant that exploits duality for correction of accumulated errors in the case of unsound or imprecise arithmetic. Although some tools favor unsound implementations [13], there are numerous use-cases where the need for soundness prohibits the use of floating-point arithmetic.

Two solutions have arisen to address this problem. The first one [26] uses a fast floating-point based implementation of simplex to traverse the vertices of a polyhedron and then follows the selected pivots by using sound rational arithmetic along the same path. If the fast method produces a wrong result, the rational simplex continues its computation (thus losing the speed advantage) until it finds the correct solution.

The second method [7] uses interval arithmetic in Fourier-Motzkin elimination to over-approximate the solution for abstract polyhedra domains. Since abstract domains are typically over-approximations of the concrete domains they abstract, exact solutions are not necessary, and these over-approximations are acceptable. These two methods show an improvement in speed performance three- to ten-fold, in most case studies. However, the analysis done in [29] shows that for a large number of real-world programs evaluated by openSMT, using an unsound floating-point simplex is marginally faster (13%) than the exact rational simplex. This is due to some optimizations in the handling of rationals inside the SMT solver and the fact that most benchmarked cases do not require higher precision arithmetic. However, we are interested in optimality as opposed to feasibility, which due to the larger number of pivots is likely trigger this case more frequently. For this reason, many of the methods and analyses presented for the SMT case are not necessarily well-suited for our use-case.

The algorithm in [15] provides an alternative: an iterative refinement method provides means to select the precision of the result arbitrarily. While this does not directly imply soundness, it can provide alternatives for δ−checks to ensure it, though as all previously mentioned papers, it only addresses the problem of floating-point rounding errors. One of the problems presented here is that there are cases where imprecision appears even before calling the decision procedure. In the case of polyhedral abstractions, linear transformations may cause the numerical representations to grow in the rationals long before the objective function is called. We particularly refer to dynamics where primal components such as eigenvalues are extracted using numerical algorithms with bounded errors which are therefore present at their injection on the simplex. Similarly, there are cases where the actual program will have limitations in the representation of certain numbers which must be evaluated as small intervals. While a precise simplex is capable of performing such operations, the combinatorial explosion can render the problem intractable, and the use of an interval floating point simplex is evidently more efficient.

Error bounds for linear and mixed integer programming have been researched in [28]. The authors make use of interval arithmetic, and more specifically rounding modes, to find error bounds on optimal outcomes of the problem. Their approach allows the use of off-the-shelf algorithms for solving a linear problem using pre- and post-processing to deal with the errors. Unfortunately, this approach excludes the possibility of missing pivots, which means that the maximal vertex may not be reached. This can cause an unnecessarily large error bound to be discovered due to the symmetry in their calculation. Additionally, they do not address problems where the statement is already in interval form due to pre-transformations. To the best of the authors' knowledge, there are no existing techniques for sound numerical analysis in a polyhedral domain suitable for dealing with pre-existing errors in pipelined modular processes.

In addition to the linear programming operations, we note that many reachability tools depend on eigen-analysis to find solutions [6,13,21]. In fact, tools that verify continuous systems through discretization require such a component. Numerical analysis offers an incredible increase in speed performance. With respect to the eigen-decomposition itself, the most common approaches to estimating the error are those implemented in LAPACK [1]. These are based on the separation between eigenvalues and offer moderately tight bounds for both eigenvalues and eigenvectors. They do not however deal well with multiplicity since the formulas depend on condition numbers which become increasingly large when the gap between two eigenvalues is small. A formal approach to eigenvalues with algebraic multiplicities is offered by [32]. The authors provide a sound algorithm for finding the boundaries of both eigenvalues and eigenvectors based on an iterative estimation of the sub-eigenvector matrix relating to a cluster of eigenvalues. Their main limitation lies in the fact that the iterations are computationally as expensive as finding the estimations themselves, which is not a bad tradeoff. Since these values are often very small (typically insignificant with respect to other over-approximation errors), we choose speed over precision, and may compensate by using more precise data types at a lower time cost overall.

4   Abstract Acceleration

The problem statement we use to drive our discussion is that of Abstract Acceleration [6,21]. Given an iterative program with dynamics

$$\boldsymbol{x}_{k+1} = \boldsymbol{A}\boldsymbol{x}_k : \boldsymbol{x}_k \in \mathbb{R}^n \wedge \boldsymbol{A} \in \mathbb{R}^{n \times n} \wedge k \in [0 \ \ \infty[, \tag{10}$$

we want to find all possible states visited over an infinite time horizon starting at an initial set X_0. We call this set the *reach tube* of the model:

$$\hat{X} = \{\boldsymbol{x}_k : k \in [0 \ \infty[\wedge \boldsymbol{x}_0 \in X_0 \wedge \boldsymbol{x}_{k+1} = \boldsymbol{A}\boldsymbol{x}_k\}. \tag{11}$$

It is easy to see that the infinite number of iterations would result in an unbounded cumulative rounding error, but using Abstract Acceleration we transform this problem into a one-step solution. We first change the problem statement by means of acceleration into

$$\hat{X} = \{\boldsymbol{x}_k = \boldsymbol{A}^k \boldsymbol{x}_0 : k \in [0 \ \infty) \wedge \boldsymbol{x}_0 \in X_0\}, \tag{12}$$

and further define new model semantics and corresponding set:

$$\hat{X} \subseteq \hat{X}^\sharp = \mathcal{A}X_0, \text{ such that } \bigcup_{k \in [0 \ \infty[} \boldsymbol{A}^k \subseteq \mathcal{A}. \tag{13}$$

where the newly introduced *abstract reach tube* $\hat{X}^\sharp$ is an over-approximation of the reach tube of the model [21]. All we need to do is define the nature of $\mathcal{A}X_0$.

Let $\boldsymbol{S}\boldsymbol{J}\boldsymbol{S}^{-1} = \boldsymbol{A}$ be the eigen-decomposition of $\boldsymbol{A}$, where $\boldsymbol{S}$ is the set of generalised eigenvectors of $\boldsymbol{A}$ and $\boldsymbol{J}$ is the Jordan form containing the eigenvalues of A in its main diagonal. We correspondingly define $\mathcal{J} = S^{-1}AS$, which is such that $\mathcal{J} \supseteq \bigcup_{k \in [0 \ \infty)} J^k$.

Given a set $X = \{x : Cx \leq d\}$. The linear transformation $x' = S^{-1}x$ leads to set

$$X' = S^{-1}X = \{x' : CSx' \leq d\}. \tag{14}$$

Analogously, let $X'_0 = S^{-1}X_0$ and $\hat{X}'^{\sharp} = S^{-1}\hat{X}^{\sharp}$ be the initial set and the abstract reach tube mapped onto the eigenspace of matrix A. We may transform Eq. (13) into:

$$\hat{X}' \subseteq \hat{X}'^{\sharp} = \mathcal{J}X'_0, \text{ such that } \bigcup_{k \in [0 \ \infty)} J^k \subseteq \mathcal{J}, \tag{15}$$

where $\hat{X}' = S^{-1}\hat{X}$ and $\mathcal{J}$ is a convex polyhedron representing restrictions on the eigenvalues of A. $\hat{X}'^{\sharp}$ is calculated by applying a simplex algorithm with a tableau defined by $\mathcal{J}$ and objective functions derived from each vertex of X'_0 (step 10 in Algorithm 1 below). We note, however, that if we wish to use numerical analysis in the decomposition of A, the Tableau in $\mathcal{J}$ contains small intervals given by the errors, which cannot be processed efficiently by a regular simplex and require a new procedure. Also note that the error bounds for S will have a similar effect on the objective functions.

The calculation of the abstract reach tube via abstract acceleration is encompassed in Algorithm 1, which can be summarised as follows (its steps are denoted in parentheses):

1. We perform unsound eigen-decomposition using an existing algebra package (lines 2–3).
2. Then we restore soundness to the results using the methods described in Sect. 5.2 (lines 4–5).
3. The inverse of the matrix of eigenvectors is calculated after soundness is restored, using interval arithmetic in order to ensure its soundness (line 6).
4. The abstract dynamics are obtained by evaluating the convex hull of all powers of eigenvalues up to the desired number of iterations as described in [6] (line 7).
5. Using Eq. (14), transform the initial state into the eigenspace (line 8).
6. Extract the vertices of the eigen-polyhedron X'_0 using the sound over-approximation of the double description algorithm [14] from Sect. 5.4 (line 9). It is worth noting that this algorithm uses a simplex to seed it: we will first discuss the simplex algorithm, which is also needed at the next step, and then the vertex enumeration algorithm used at this stage.
7. Calculate the mapped *abstract reach tube* $\hat{X}'^{\sharp}$ that over-approximates the image of the reach tube in the eigenspace (line 10). This is achieved by evaluating a set of objective functions using the abstract dynamics as a simplex Tableau, and via a sound simplex described in Sect. 5.3. The objective functions are defined by the vertices of X'_0, denoted as V_0, and by the desired template directions, such that

$$w_{ij} = v_i \circ t_j : v_i \in V_0 \wedge t_j \in T,$$

where T is the set of template directions, and $\circ$ denotes a component-wise multiplication yielding a vector.

8. Using Eq. (14), find the reach tube $\hat{X}^\sharp = S\hat{X}'^\sharp$ (line 11).

Algorithm 1. Calculation of Abstract Reach Tube Using Abstract Acceleration

---

Input: $X_0 A, k.$
Output: $\hat{X}^\sharp$
1: **function** *findAbstractReachTube*()
2:     $\hat{J}$ = calculateEigenvalues(A)
3:     $\hat{S}$ = calculateEigenvectors(A)
4:     $[J]$ = soundifyEigenvalues($A, \hat{J}, \hat{S}$)
5:     $[S]$ = soundifyEigenvectors($A, [J], \hat{S}$)
6:     $[S]^{-1}$ = calculateInverse($[S]$)
7:     $\mathcal{J}$ = getAbstractDynamics($[J]$)
8:     $[X_0']$ = transformInitialSpace($X_0, [S]^{-1}$)
9:     $[V_0]$ = getVertices($[X_0']$)
10:     $\hat{X}'^\sharp$ = getReachTube($\mathcal{J}, [V_0]$)
11:     $\hat{X}^\sharp$ = transformReachTube($\hat{X}'^\sharp, [S]$)
12: **end function**

---

5   Implementation

5.1   An Interval Partial Order for Vector Spaces

Interval arithmetic is widely researched and used in the literature. The main issue in its implementation here is with respect to ordering, since some of the operations used require ordered sets. While real numbers have a well defined order, there are several different options regarding the order of real intervals. This creates a problem for programs dealing with branching since an incorrect assumption on the order will cause undetermined behaviour. The reader is referred to literature [5,9–11] for possible orderings of real intervals. In this paper, we have selected the following paradigm:

Let $[x] = [\underline{x}\ \overline{x}]$ be an interval of real numbers such that

$$\begin{cases} [x] < 0 & \overline{x} < 0 \\ [x] > 0 & \underline{x} > 0 \\ [x] = 0 & -e \le \underline{x} \le 0 \wedge 0 \le \overline{x} \le e \\ [x] \text{ is deemed imprecise} & \underline{x} < -e \wedge \overline{x} \ge 0 \vee \underline{x} \le 0 \wedge \overline{x} > e, \end{cases} \tag{16}$$

where e is a user-defined error bound.

The first two definitions correspond to precedence definitions in the IEEE standard, but the third one is an enabling comparison (*i.e.* it corresponds to "may be equal to") which is not present in the standard. Throughout this work this latter definition is useful because the operations that relate to this condition have no negative effect if applied when the condition is false (apart from the increased processing time of the operation), nor do they compromise soundness.

Imprecise numbers break the ordering: for example, they could be originally non-zero elements whose error touches zero – while this situation does not break the soundness of the algorithms described in this paper, it affects their precision and completeness, as described in Sect. 5.3). As such, it is established that the appearance of an imprecise number forces a change in the error bound e or an increase in the precision, so that the accumulated errors do not surpass this bound (e). From the above paradigm we can easily derive that

$$\begin{cases} [x] = [y] & \iff [x] - [y] = 0 \\ [x] < [y] & \iff [x] - [y] < 0 \\ [x] > [y] & \iff [x] - [y] > 0, \end{cases} \tag{17}$$

which results in our ordering.

We will extend this definition to the dot product of two vectors, in order to establish equality in higher-dimensional spaces (in particular, this will allow us to set an ordering of value pairs). Let $\mathsf{v} = [[v_1] \cdots [v_n]]^T$ and $\mathsf{u} = [[u_1] \cdots [u_n]]^T$ be interval column vectors, with $[d] = \mathsf{v} \cdot \mathsf{u}$, then we say that

$$\begin{cases} \mathsf{v} \cdot \mathsf{u} < 0 & \overline{d} < 0 \\ \mathsf{v} \cdot \mathsf{u} > 0 & \underline{d} > 0 \\ \mathsf{v} \cdot \mathsf{u} = 0 & -e \leq \underline{d} \leq 0 \wedge 0 \leq \overline{d} \leq e \\ \mathsf{v} \cdot \mathsf{u} \text{ is deemed imprecise} & \text{otherwise.} \end{cases} \tag{18}$$

5.2 Eigen-Decomposition

The first stage required for Abstract Acceleration is the eigen-decomposition of the dynamics (steps 2–3 in Algorithm 1). We seek to find the Jordan form of a matrix, characterising its eigenvalues alongside their corresponding eigenvectors, with known error bounds for both. For this purpose we use the package *eigen* [17], which contains an efficient fast numerical eigensolver using Schur decomposition. The main advantage of eigen over other packages is that it is a template library which can be used with any numerical data type. Since we are interested in using multiple precision floating point integers, this is an important feature of the desired package. Unfortunately, the eigen-decomposition cannot be performed using interval arithmetic. This is because numerical solvers for this problem exploit the convergence of successive results towards a precise value. While the process is known to converge, the latter iterations will typically oscillate around the final values, which causes the interval containing the final eigenvalue to expand, resulting in a width that becomes unbounded, rather than in a small interval around the expected result. We therefore use standard arithmetics to obtain a numerical approximation of the true eigenspace, and then find error bounds using interval arithmetic to generate the intervals containing the true values in the eigenspace. Namely, we call a standard unsound eigen-decomposition algorithm, and later make it sound by creating intervals around the results using soundly-calculated error bounds.

We remark that these error bounds are found in the LAPACK [1] package, used by programs such as Matlab, and could therefore be correctly obtained by using this tool. However, four issues drive us away from LAPACK. The first is that the library is written in FORTRAN and uses double-precision floating-point arithmetic: this restricts our ability to use higher precision to obtain smaller errors. The second is that some of the procedures used in LAPACK to calculate the error can be time consuming, which can have a large impact on the overall processing time. The third one is that LAPACK does not allow the use of intervals, hence the operations that calculate the error bound have rounding errors themselves and are thus unsound. The final problem is that LAPACK does not provide Jordan forms with geometric multiplicities, nor can it always ensure the error bounds for algebraic multiplicities greater than one.

The calculation of the error bounds for soundness is performed in two stages, first for the eigenvalues and then for the eigenvectors (the latter requires the sound eigenvalue intervals in its calculation).

We first define an interval matrix, which will be used during both stages. Let

$$
\mathbb{M} \in \mathbb{R}^{p \times q} = \begin{bmatrix} [m_{11}] & \cdots & [m_{1q}] \\ \vdots & \ddots & \vdots \\ [m_{p1}] & \cdots & [m_{pq}] \end{bmatrix}, \tag{19}
$$

where $[m_{ij}] = \begin{bmatrix} \underline{m_{ij}} & \overline{m_{ij}} \end{bmatrix} : i \in [1 \ldots p] \wedge j \in [1 \ldots q]$ be an interval matrix. Interval arithmetics between interval matrices derives directly from the operations between their elements. We may trivially construct an interval equivalent of any non-interval matrix using the following definition:

$$
\mathbb{M} = \boldsymbol{M} \text{ iff } \forall [m_{ij}] \in [\boldsymbol{M}], \ \underline{m_{ij}} = \overline{m_{ij}} = m_{ij} \in \boldsymbol{M} : i \in [1 \ldots p] \wedge j \in [1 \ldots q]. \tag{20}
$$

Error Bounds on the Eigenvalues (step (4) in Algorithm 1).

Theorem 1. *Given an eigenvalue λ_i with algebraic multiplicity m_i obtained using Jordan decomposition, the error of the numerically calculated eigenvalue $\hat{\lambda}_i$ is upper bounded by the formula:*

$$
e_{\lambda_i} \leq e_{m_i} = \begin{cases} E & m_i = 1 \\ \dfrac{E^{\frac{1}{m_i}}}{1 - E^{\frac{1}{m_i}}} & m_i > 1 \end{cases}, \ \textit{where } E = \max\left(k\left(\hat{\mathbb{S}}\right) \|\hat{\mathbb{S}}\hat{\mathbb{J}}\hat{\mathbb{S}}^{-1} - \mathbb{A}\|_2 \right), \tag{21}
$$

where m_i is the geometric multiplicity of λ_i, $\hat{\mathbb{S}} = \hat{\boldsymbol{S}}$ are the calculated eigenvectors of $\boldsymbol{A}$, $\hat{\mathbb{J}} = \hat{\boldsymbol{J}}$ its calculated Jordan form and $k(\mathbb{M})$ is the condition number of a given matrix $\mathbb{M}$ that is defined as $[\sigma_{max}](\mathbb{M})/[\sigma_{min}](\mathbb{M})$, where $[\sigma_i]$ are the singular values of $\mathbb{M}$.[3] The obtained matrix $\mathbb{J} = [\hat{\boldsymbol{J}} - \sup(e_{m_i})\boldsymbol{I} \quad \hat{\boldsymbol{J}} + \sup(e_{m_i})\boldsymbol{I}] \supseteq \boldsymbol{J} : i \in [1 \ldots n]$ is a sound over-approximation of the diagonal matrix with the eigenvalues of $\boldsymbol{A}$. All matrices are in $\mathbb{R}^{n \times n}$.

---

[3] Note that this is equivalent to $k(\mathbb{M}) = \|\mathbb{M}\|_2 \|\mathbb{M}^{-1}\|_2$.

Proof. Let us first assume that matrix $\boldsymbol{A}$ is diagonalizable (an hypothesis relaxed below). Let us also define the numerically calculated approximation $\hat{\boldsymbol{A}} \simeq \boldsymbol{A}$ with Jordan form $\hat{\boldsymbol{J}}$ and eigenvectors $\hat{\boldsymbol{S}}$. Then the error bound for each of the eigenvalues is [33]:

$$e_{\lambda_i} = |\lambda_i - \hat{\lambda}_i| < k(\boldsymbol{S})\|\boldsymbol{A} - \hat{\boldsymbol{A}}\|_2 = k(\boldsymbol{S})\|\boldsymbol{A} - \hat{\boldsymbol{S}}\hat{\boldsymbol{J}}\hat{\boldsymbol{S}}^{-1}\|_2. \tag{22}$$

Note that symmetrically

$$e_{\lambda_i} = e_{\hat{\lambda}_i} = |\hat{\lambda}_i - \lambda_i| < k(\hat{\boldsymbol{S}})\|\hat{\boldsymbol{A}} - \boldsymbol{A}\|_2 = k(\hat{\boldsymbol{S}})\|\hat{\boldsymbol{S}}\hat{\boldsymbol{J}}\hat{\boldsymbol{S}}^{-1} - \boldsymbol{A}\|_2 \tag{23}$$

as long as $\hat{\boldsymbol{A}} = \hat{\boldsymbol{S}}\hat{\boldsymbol{J}}\hat{\boldsymbol{S}}^{-1}$ has no rounding errors. Therefore, to ensure soundness, we must translate the error calculation into an interval arithmetic problem.

Using (20), Eq. (23) then becomes

$$e_{\lambda_i} < \sup\left(k\left(\hat{\mathbb{S}}\right)\|\hat{\mathbb{S}}\hat{\mathbb{J}}\hat{\mathbb{S}}^{-1} - \mathbb{A}\|_2\right).$$

For simplicity, we will hereon use $\hat{\mathbb{A}} = \hat{\mathbb{S}}\hat{\mathbb{J}}\hat{\mathbb{S}}^{-1}$.

We could calculate tighter bounds for each eigenvalue using the condition number of individual eigenvectors (which is defined for non-square matrices as $k(\boldsymbol{M}) = \|\boldsymbol{M}\|_2\|\boldsymbol{M}^+\|_2$, where $\boldsymbol{M}^+$ is the pseudo-inverse of $\boldsymbol{M}$), but we choose this faster approach expecting the increased error to be negligible with respect to the dynamics.

Extending our analysis by relaxing the assumption made above, when there exists a Jordan block in $\boldsymbol{A}$ with geometric multiplicity m_i, then the error can be derived by leveraging [33] as follows:

$$\frac{|\lambda_i - \hat{\lambda}_i|^{m_i}}{(1+|\lambda_i - \hat{\lambda}_i|)^{m_i - 1}} = (1 + |\lambda_i - \hat{\lambda}_i|)\left(\frac{|\lambda_i - \hat{\lambda}_i|}{(1+|\lambda_i - \hat{\lambda}_i|)}\right)^{m_i} < k(\hat{\boldsymbol{S}})\|\hat{\boldsymbol{S}}\hat{\boldsymbol{J}}\hat{\boldsymbol{S}}^{-1} - \boldsymbol{A}\|_2$$

$$\Rightarrow \frac{|\lambda_i - \hat{\lambda}_i|}{(1+|\lambda_i - \hat{\lambda}_i|)} < \left(k(\hat{\boldsymbol{S}})\|\hat{\boldsymbol{S}}\hat{\boldsymbol{J}}\hat{\boldsymbol{S}}^{-1} - \boldsymbol{A}\|_2\right)^{\frac{1}{m_i}} < \sup\left(k(\hat{\mathbb{S}})\|\hat{\mathbb{A}} - \mathbb{A}\|_2\right)^{\frac{1}{m_i}}$$

$$\Rightarrow e_{\lambda_i} < \sup\left(\frac{\left(k(\hat{\mathbb{S}})\|\hat{\mathbb{A}} - \mathbb{A}\|_2\right)^{\frac{1}{m_i}}}{1 - \left(k(\hat{\mathbb{S}})\|\hat{\mathbb{A}} - \mathbb{A}\|_2\right)^{\frac{1}{m_i}}}\right).$$

However, this bound requires that the correct Jordan shape be selected (i.e., the one that corresponds to the original dynamics without numerical errors), which means we need to use the formula using the largest possible Jordan block for each set of similar λ (i.e., eigenvalues which intersect given their error intervals). In fact, this is not enough to ensure the bound since different shapes will result in different condition numbers (since they will have different generalized eigenvectors), so we are forced to calculate the maximum bound for all options. We will see later how to overcome this difficulty in a more efficient way. □

Now that we can obtain sound eigenvalues, we will proceed to restore soundness to the eigenvectors.

Error Bounds on the Eigenvectors (step 5 in Algorithm 1).

Theorem 2. *The interval eigenvector*

$$\mathsf{v}_i = \left[\hat{\mathsf{v}}_i \cos([\theta]_i) \quad \frac{\hat{\mathsf{v}}_i}{\cos([\theta]_i)} \right] \supseteq v_i, \ where \tag{24}$$

$$[\theta]_i \leq [\hat{\theta}]_i = \left(\frac{n}{n-1} \right)^{\frac{n-1}{2}} \frac{\|A - \hat{A}\|_2 \, (n\|U - [\lambda_i]I\|_2)^{n-1}}{n^{\frac{n}{2}} \prod_{i \neq j} ([\lambda_j] - [\lambda_i])^{m_i}} : [\hat{\theta}]_i < \frac{\pi}{2}$$

is an over-approximation of the true eigenvector v_i. Here, n is the dimension of A, m_i is the size of the ith Jordan block of A, $\hat{\mathsf{v}}_i = \hat{v}_i$ the numerically calculated i^{th} eigenvector of A, $[\lambda_i]$ the error-bound interval for the ith eigenvalue of A (inherited from above), and $U = Q^{-1}AQ$ where $Q = Q$ the Schur decomposition of A.

Given sufficient precision in the numerical calculations, we have that $[\hat{\theta}]_i < \frac{\pi}{2}$. This inequality can always be obtained by increasing precision.

Proof. The error angle between the numerically calculated i^{th} eigenvector and the true i^{th} eigenvector of A is

$$\theta_i = \cos^{-1}(v_i \cdot \hat{v}_i) < \frac{\|A - \hat{S}\hat{J}\hat{S}^{-1}\|_2}{sep_i} : \|v_i\|_2 = \|\hat{v}_i\|_2 = 1, \tag{25}$$

where v_i is the original i^{th} eigenvector, $\hat{v}_i$ is the numerically calculated eigenvector, and sep_i is the separation between Jordan blocks, which is calculated as follows.

Let U be an upper triangular matrix such that $AQ = QU$ with Q a unitary matrix ($Q^{-1} = Q^*$). This is the Schur decomposition of A. The eigenvalues of A are the diagonal entries of U. There are $s!$ different matrices U (where s is the number of Jordan blocks) corresponding to all possible permutations of the eigenvalues of A in the diagonal. Let

$$U = \begin{bmatrix} U_{11} & U_{12} \\ 0 & U_{22} \end{bmatrix}, U_{11} \in \mathbb{R}^{m \times m}, U_{22} \in \mathbb{R}^{(n-m) \times (n-m)},$$

such that the eigenvalues of U_{11} are the eigenvalues of the ith Jordan block of $A, J_i \in \mathbb{R}^{m \times m}$. The separation sep_i of J_i is the smallest difference between any singular value of U_{11} and those of U_{22} [36]. This value can be obtained by computing the smallest singular value of the Kronecker product [22]

$$K = U_{11} \otimes I_{(n-m),(n-m)} - I_{m,m} \otimes U_{22}.$$

However, this computation is expensive. Moreover, a permutation of the matrix U must be executed for each different eigenvalue of U. Hence, we look for a solution that avoids computing these values altogether.

First we will find a lower bound for the separation, which can be obtained by applying [18] to the Kronecker product K:

$$\sigma_{min}(K) \geq \left(\frac{p-1}{p}\right)^{\frac{p-1}{2}} \det(K) \min\left(\frac{c_{min}}{\prod_1^p c_j}, \frac{r_{min}}{\prod_1^p r_j}\right) : K \in \mathbb{R}^{p\times p}, p = m(n-m), \tag{26}$$

where n is the dimension of the original matrix, m is the dimension of the current Jordan block, c_j is the 2-norm of the jth column of K and r_j the 2-norm of the jth row (with corresponding minima c_{min}, r_{min}).

Let us first look at the case of matrices with all eigenvalues having algebraic multiplicity of 1 (we'll use the apex i to indicate a partition of U relating to the ith Jordan block). In this case $U^i_{11} = \lambda_i$ and, since K^i is an upper triangular matrix and its determinant is therefore the product of its diagonal entries,

$$det(K^i) = \prod_{i\neq j}(\lambda_j - \lambda_i).$$

We also note that

$$\sum_1^p c_j^2 = \|K^i\|_2^2 \wedge \sum_1^p r_j^2 = \|K^i\|_2^2.$$

Using the arithmetic and geometric mean inequality [35] we have

$$\prod_{j=1}^p c_j \leq \left(\frac{1}{p}\right)^{\frac{p}{2}}\|K^i\|_2^p \wedge \prod_{j=1}^p r_j \leq \left(\frac{1}{p}\right)^{\frac{p}{2}}\|K^i\|_2^p,$$

where $\|K^i\|_2 = \|U^i_{22} - \lambda_i I\|_2 \leq \|U - \lambda_i I\|_2$.

Finally, given that for any matrix U^i_{11} we can select any permutation of U^i_{22} such that the first element of K^i is $\min_{i\neq j}(\lambda_j - \lambda_i)$ and given that K^i is upper triangular, this means that $c_{min} = \min_{i\neq j}(\lambda_j - \lambda_i) \leq r_{min}$.

Going back to Eq. (26), we have:

$$\sigma_{min}(K^i) \geq \left(\frac{p-1}{p}\right)^{\frac{p-1}{2}} \frac{\prod_{i\neq j}(\lambda_j - \lambda_i)}{\left(\frac{1}{p}\right)^{\frac{p}{2}}\|U - \lambda_i I\|_2^{p-1}}.$$

This term neither depends on the calculation of K, nor on the ordering of U.

In the case of a matrix U with algebraic multiplicity strictly greater than one, we should remark that the matrix K has dimension $m(n-m)$. Its determinant is

$$\det(K^i) = \left(\prod_{i\neq j}(\lambda_j - \lambda_i)\right)^m$$

and its norm is

$$\|K^i\|_2 \leq m\|U^i_{22} - \lambda_i I\|_2 + (n-m)\|U^i_{11} - \lambda_i I\|_2 \leq n\|U - \lambda_i I\|_2,$$

therefore

$$\sigma_{min}(\boldsymbol{K}^i) \geq \left(\frac{n-1}{n}\right)^{\frac{n-1}{2}} \frac{\left(\prod_{i\neq j}(\lambda_j - \lambda_i)\right)^m}{\left(\frac{1}{n}\right)^{\frac{n}{2}}(n\|\boldsymbol{U} - \lambda_i\boldsymbol{I}\|_2)^{n-1}}.$$

Replacing for (25) and using interval arithmetic we get Eq. (24). The last part of the equation comes from the need for the cosine to be positive. In practice we want a much smaller number, so if θ_i is too large, then we can report that the result is imprecise and require the use of higher precision.   □

Error Bounds for Unknown Jordan Shapes. As stated earlier, the preceding discussion relies on having selected the correct Jordan shape in the first place (that is, the Jordan shape for the theoretical decomposition without calculation errors), which is in most cases unverifiable. This means that our solution thus far can only be fully sound for diagonalisable matrices (i.e., if the separation of the eigenvalues is larger than the error) or those where the Jordan shape is known a-priori. We therefore propose an additional mechanism to deal with the case of non-diagonalisable matrices with unknown Jordan shapes. In the following, the symbol $\mathbf{1} = \begin{bmatrix} 1 \cdots 1 \\ \vdots \ddots \vdots \\ 1 \cdots 1 \end{bmatrix}$ represents a appropriately-sized matrix with elements all equal to one.

Theorem 3. *Given a numerical decomposition of* $\boldsymbol{A}$, $\hat{\boldsymbol{A}} = \hat{\boldsymbol{S}}\hat{\boldsymbol{J}}\hat{\boldsymbol{S}}^{-1}$, *the interval matrix*

$$\mathbb{A}'_k = \hat{\mathbb{S}}'\hat{\mathbb{J}}'_k\hat{\mathbb{S}}'^{-1} : \hat{\mathbb{J}}'_k = \hat{\boldsymbol{J}}^k + ((\|\hat{\boldsymbol{J}}\|_1 + [e])^k - \|\hat{\boldsymbol{J}}\|_1^k) \ and \ \hat{\mathbb{S}}' = \hat{\boldsymbol{S}}(\boldsymbol{I} + [e]\mathbf{1}) \ (27)$$

where $[e] = [-e \ e]$ *and* $e = \max(n, \|\hat{\boldsymbol{J}}\|)\|\hat{\boldsymbol{S}}^{-1}\boldsymbol{A}\hat{\boldsymbol{S}} - \hat{\boldsymbol{J}}\|_2$, *is an overapproximation of* $\boldsymbol{A}^k$.

Proof. Let

$$\hat{\boldsymbol{S}}^{-1}\boldsymbol{A}\hat{\boldsymbol{S}} = \hat{\boldsymbol{J}} + \boldsymbol{J}_e \Leftrightarrow \boldsymbol{A} = \hat{\boldsymbol{S}}(\hat{\boldsymbol{J}} + \boldsymbol{J}_e)\hat{\boldsymbol{S}}^{-1},$$

where $\boldsymbol{J}_e = \hat{\boldsymbol{S}}^{-1}\boldsymbol{A}\hat{\boldsymbol{S}} - \hat{\boldsymbol{J}}$ is an error matrix computed from the known quantities on the RHS of the equation. Then

$$\boldsymbol{A}^k = \hat{\boldsymbol{S}}(\hat{\boldsymbol{J}} + \boldsymbol{J}_e)^k\hat{\boldsymbol{S}}^{-1}. \tag{28}$$

Let $[e'] = [-\|\boldsymbol{J}_e\|_1 \ \|\boldsymbol{J}_e\|_1]$ and $\mathbb{J}'_e = [e']\mathbf{1}$, then $\boldsymbol{J}_e \subseteq \mathbb{J}'_e$.

Since each element of $\mathbb{J}'_e$ is $[e']$, each element in $\mathbb{J}'^k_e$ will be $n^{k-1}[e']^k = (n\|\boldsymbol{J}_e\|_1)^{k-1}[e']$, therefore $\mathbb{J}'^k_e = (n\|\boldsymbol{J}_e\|_1)^{k-1}[\mathbb{J}'_e]$. Similarly, $\mathbb{J}'_e\hat{\boldsymbol{J}}^k\mathbb{J}'_e \subseteq \|\boldsymbol{J}_e\|_1 \|\hat{\boldsymbol{J}}\|_1^k\mathbb{J}'_e$.

Let $[e] = \max(n, \|\hat{\boldsymbol{J}}\|_1)[e'] \wedge \mathbb{J}_e = [e]\mathbf{1}$, so that $(n\|\boldsymbol{J}_e\|_1)^{k-1}\mathbb{J}'_e \subseteq ([e])^{k-1}[\mathbb{J}'_e] \wedge \|\boldsymbol{J}_e\|_1\|\hat{\boldsymbol{J}}\|_1\mathbb{J}'_e \subseteq [e]\mathbb{J}'_e$. More generally any matrix multiplication with i elements $\hat{\boldsymbol{J}}$ and j elements $\mathbb{J}'_e$ may be overapproximated by

$[e]^{j-1}\|\hat{\boldsymbol{J}}\|_1^i\,\mathbb{J}'_e \subseteq [e]^j\|\hat{\boldsymbol{J}}\|_1^i\mathbf{1}$. From the above properties we expand (28) replacing for these values and obtain:

$$A^k \subseteq \hat{\boldsymbol{S}}\left(\hat{\boldsymbol{J}}^k + \sum_{i=0}^{k-1}\binom{k}{i}[e]^{k-i}\|\hat{\boldsymbol{J}}\|_1^i\mathbf{1}\right)\hat{\boldsymbol{S}}^{-1} \tag{29}$$

$$\Rightarrow A^k \subseteq \hat{\boldsymbol{S}}\left(\hat{\boldsymbol{J}}^k - \|\hat{\boldsymbol{J}}\|_1^k + \sum_{i=0}^{k}\binom{k}{i}[e]^{k-i}\|\hat{\boldsymbol{J}}\|_1^i\mathbf{1}\right)\hat{\boldsymbol{S}}^{-1}$$

$$\Rightarrow A^k \subseteq \hat{\boldsymbol{S}}\left(\hat{\boldsymbol{J}}^k + ((\|\hat{\boldsymbol{J}}\|_1 + [e])^k - \|\hat{\boldsymbol{J}}\|_1^k)\mathbf{1}\right)\hat{\boldsymbol{S}}^{-1}$$

$$\Rightarrow A^k \subseteq \hat{\boldsymbol{S}}(I + \mathbb{J}_e)\left(\hat{\boldsymbol{J}}^k + ((\|\hat{\boldsymbol{J}}\|_1 + [e])^k - \|\hat{\boldsymbol{J}}\|_1^k)\right)\hat{\boldsymbol{S}}^{-1}.$$

$\square$

Notice that, since the formula depends on the horizon k, we cannot in general prove soundness for an unbounded time horizon in this case. In the instance of converging models (as is often the case for industrial systems), we may pick a k that practically reaches a fix point in finite time, thus extending the proof for an infinite time horizon.

5.3 Interval Simplex

The key implementation required for the Algorithm (step 10 in Algorithm 1) is a variant of simplex that can handle interval representations. We first remark that throughout this paper we are looking at over-approximations of desired quantities in order to ensure soundness, and to optimise algorithmic performance. Let us begin by exploring the meaning of a polyhedral description using interval inequalities. An interval polyhedron $[P] = \{\boldsymbol{x} : \mathbb{A}\boldsymbol{x} \le \mathbb{b}\}$ is a union of polyhedra such that

$$[P] = \bigcup P_i : P_i = \{\boldsymbol{x} : A_i\boldsymbol{x} \le b_i\}, A_i \in \mathbb{A} \wedge b_i \in \mathbb{b}. \tag{30}$$

Note that $[P]$ is not guaranteed to be convex even if all P_i are. We begin by simplifying this description.

Theorem 4. *The polyhedron*

$$\hat{P}_i = \left\{\boldsymbol{x} : A_i\boldsymbol{x} \le \hat{b} \wedge A_i \in \mathbb{A} \wedge \hat{b}^j = \overline{b^j}\right\}, \tag{31}$$

where $\mathbb{b}^j$ is the jth row of $\mathbb{b}$ and $\overline{b^j} = \sup(\mathbb{b}^j)$, is a sound over-approximation of P_i.

Proof. Let $\boldsymbol{r}_i^j$ be a row in A_i with $\rho_{P_i}(\boldsymbol{r}_i^j) = b_i^j$ its corresponding support function. Eqs. (30) and (31) state that

$$\boldsymbol{x} \in P_i \Leftrightarrow \forall j,\ \boldsymbol{r}_i^j\boldsymbol{x} \le b_i^j \ \wedge\ \boldsymbol{x} \in \hat{P}_i \Leftrightarrow \forall j,\ \boldsymbol{r}_i^j\boldsymbol{x} \le \hat{b}^j. \tag{32}$$

Since $\forall i,\ \boldsymbol{b}_i^j \leq \overline{\boldsymbol{b}^j} \wedge \overline{\boldsymbol{b}^j} = \hat{\boldsymbol{b}}^j$, we have that

$$x \in P_i \Rightarrow \forall j,\ \boldsymbol{r}_i^j \boldsymbol{x} \leq \hat{\boldsymbol{b}}^j \Rightarrow \boldsymbol{x} \in \hat{P}_i \Rightarrow P_i \subseteq \hat{P}_i. \qquad (33)$$

The above equation shows that $\hat{P}_i$ is an over-approximation of the polyhedron P_i obtained by relaxing the support functions to the upper limit of their intervals.   □

Using Theorem 4, we reduce the description of the Abstract Polyhedron to $[P] = \bigcup \hat{P}_i$.

The standard (non-interval) simplex algorithm visits a sequence of contiguous vertices $\boldsymbol{p}_i^p \in P_i$ and computes the *support function* of the last point $\boldsymbol{p}_i^n$ in this sequence in the direction of the objective function $\boldsymbol{v}$ (i.e., $\boldsymbol{v} \cdot \boldsymbol{p}_i^n$). Hence, to develop an interval simplex we need to describe the vertices of $[P]$ in a way that can be traversed and yields a solution $[\boldsymbol{v}] \cdot \mathbb{p}^n$.

Definition 4. *An extreme point of a polyhedron P is any point in the polyhedron touching at least one of its faces. Let $\boldsymbol{A}_i^p$ be a subset of rows of $\boldsymbol{A}_i$ with $\hat{\boldsymbol{b}}^p$ a subset of the corresponding rows in $\hat{\boldsymbol{b}}$ and $\boldsymbol{A}_i^{/p} \wedge \hat{\boldsymbol{b}}^{/p}$ their complementary rows and vector elements, respectively. An extreme point $\hat{\boldsymbol{p}}_i^p$ is defined by the equation:*

$$\boldsymbol{A}_i^p \hat{\boldsymbol{p}}_i^p = \hat{\boldsymbol{b}}^p \wedge \boldsymbol{A}_i^{/p} \hat{\boldsymbol{p}}_i^p \leq \hat{\boldsymbol{b}}^{/p}. \qquad (34)$$

Definition 5. *A vertex of a polyhedron P is an extreme point in the polyhedron touching as many faces as the dimension of the polyhedron, namely*

$$\boldsymbol{A}_i^p \hat{\boldsymbol{p}}_i^p = \hat{\boldsymbol{b}}^p \wedge \boldsymbol{A}_i^{/p} \hat{\boldsymbol{p}}_i^p < \hat{\boldsymbol{b}}^{/p} : \hat{\boldsymbol{p}}_i^p \in \mathbb{R}^n \wedge |p| = n. \qquad (35)$$

where $|p|$ represents the number of rows in $\boldsymbol{A}_i^p$.

Definition 6. *An abstract vertex $\mathbb{p}^p \in [P]$ is a hyperbox containing a corresponding vertex for each polyhedron in the collection $\hat{\boldsymbol{p}}_i^p \in \hat{P}_i$, so that $\mathbb{p}^p \supseteq Conv\left(\bigcup_i \hat{\boldsymbol{p}}_i^p\right)$. In the following we will replace the index p representing the basis of the vertex with the index k representing the order in which vertices are visited. For a visual representation, see Fig. 1, where each set of halfplanes $\boldsymbol{r}_i^j \boldsymbol{x} \leq \hat{\boldsymbol{b}}^j$ (sets of lines marked $j = 1, 2, 3$ where each line represents the index i) intesects with another at an abstract vertex $\mathbb{p}^p$ (boxes). We can find multiple intersections inside each box corresponding to $\hat{\boldsymbol{p}}_i^p$.*

Definition 7. *A basis $\boldsymbol{B} \in \mathbb{R}^{n \times n}$ is a set of independent vectors, the linear combination of which spans the space $\mathbb{R}^n$.*

Theorem 5. *Given a pivot operation $pv\left(\boldsymbol{p}_i^k, \boldsymbol{p}_i^{k+1}\right) : \boldsymbol{p}_i^k \to \boldsymbol{p}_i^{k+1}$, an abstract pivot is a transformation*

$$pv\left(\mathbb{p}^k, \mathbb{p}^{k+1}\right) : \forall i,\ \hat{\boldsymbol{p}}_i^k \in \mathbb{p}^k \to \hat{\boldsymbol{p}}_i^{k+1} \in \mathbb{p}^{k+1}. \qquad (36)$$

Notice that the pivot can be performed on any point, thus it is not limited to vertices or points within the polyhedron (this allows our abstract pivot to take effect on all points in the hyperbox of the abstract vertex).

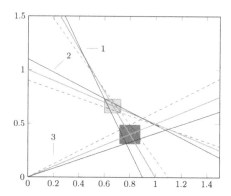

Fig. 1. Three interval half-planes with negative (dashed red), zero (thick green) and positive (thin blue) angular error representations. The yellow and orange areas (hypercubes) over-approximate all possible vertices of the resulting polyhedron at the given location. If these hypercubes partially intersect, the abstract vertex $\mathbb{p}^k$ must necessarily contain all intersecting hypercubes. (Color figure online)

Proof. Let $\boldsymbol{B}_i^k$ be a basis for $\hat{P}_i$ related to point $\boldsymbol{p}_i^k$, and such that

$$A_i \boldsymbol{p}_i^k + \boldsymbol{B}_i^k \boldsymbol{s}_i^k = \hat{\boldsymbol{b}}, \tag{37}$$

where s_i^k is a set of auxiliary variables [4]. The pivot operation $pv\left(\boldsymbol{p}_i^k, \boldsymbol{p}_i^{k+1}\right)$ will change the basis such that $\boldsymbol{B}_i^{k+1} = \left(\boldsymbol{E}^k\right)^{-1} \boldsymbol{B}_i^k$. We therefore have

$$A_i \boldsymbol{p}_i^k + \boldsymbol{B}_i^k \boldsymbol{s}_i^k = A_i \boldsymbol{p}_i^{k+1} + \boldsymbol{B}_i^{k+1} \boldsymbol{s}_i^{k+1} = A_i \boldsymbol{p}_i^{k+1} + \left(\boldsymbol{E}^k\right)^{-1} \boldsymbol{B}_i^k \boldsymbol{s}_i^{k+1} \tag{38}$$

$$\Rightarrow \boldsymbol{B}_i^k \boldsymbol{s}_i^k = A_i \left(\boldsymbol{p}_i^{k+1} - \boldsymbol{p}_i^k\right) + \left(\boldsymbol{E}^k\right)^{-1} \boldsymbol{B}_i^k \boldsymbol{s}_i^{k+1}.$$

The reason for using the inverse of $\boldsymbol{E}^k$ in the last equation is because implementations of the simplex often work on the inverse of the basis and the formula is not commutative using interval arithmetic. Since $\boldsymbol{E}^k$ creates a change between two bases spanning the same space, it is invertible.

Let $\mathbb{B}^k \supseteq \bigcup_i \boldsymbol{B}_i^k$ be an overapproximation of the basis related to $\mathbb{p}^k \in [P]$ (*i.e.* the set of bases relating to each point in $\mathbb{p}^k$). An abstract pivot preserves the over-approximation of the bases in Eqs. (36) and (38) since:

$$\forall k, \exists \mathbb{E}^k \supseteq \bigcup_i E_i^k : \mathbb{B}^{k+1} = \left(\mathbb{E}^k\right)^{-1} \mathbb{B}^k \supseteq \bigcup_i \boldsymbol{B}_i^{k+1}. \tag{39}$$

Applying interval arithmetic to Eq. (38) and moving $\mathbb{A}$ to the right, we obtain:

$$\left(\mathbb{E}^k\right)^{-1} \mathbb{B}^k \mathbb{s}^{k+1} \supseteq \mathbb{A} \left(\mathbb{p}^k - \mathbb{p}^{k+1}\right) + \mathbb{B}^k \mathbb{s}^k \tag{40}$$

$$\Rightarrow \forall i, \left(\mathbb{E}^k\right)^{-1} \boldsymbol{B}_i^k \boldsymbol{s}_i^{k+1} \supseteq A_i \left(\boldsymbol{p}_i^k - \boldsymbol{p}_i^{k+1}\right) + \boldsymbol{B}_i^k \boldsymbol{s}_i^k.$$

Equations (39) and (40) are satisfiable if we pick large enough intervals for the elements of $\mathbb{E}^k$, thus proving the theorem. $\square$

A new problem arises regarding precision: whereas before we had disjoint vertices $\boldsymbol{p}^k \neq \boldsymbol{p}^{k+1}$, we now have possible intersections $\mathbb{p}^k \cap \mathbb{p}^{k+1} \neq \oslash$. There are three consequences.

First, the over-approximation may become highly imprecise. Second, the algorithm may start cycling between the two intersecting vertices, which may cause the program to not terminate. While imprecision has been defined in Eq. (16), the question is how to show completeness. We consider the definition of the vertices and Eq. (18). If $\mathbb{A}\mathbb{p}^k$ is imprecise, then the base $\mathbb{B}^k$ is incomplete, and we abort the simplex, indicating that higher precision is required.

The third effect is that the corresponding confusion between two bases may cause the simplex to pivot erroneously on the second basis (i.e., once a vertex $\mathbb{p}^{k+1}$ is reached, the next pivot may start from $\mathbb{p}^j : \mathbb{p}^j \cap \mathbb{p}^{k+1} \neq \oslash$ where $\exists i : \boldsymbol{A}_i \boldsymbol{p}_i^j + \boldsymbol{B}_i^{k+1} \boldsymbol{s}_i^{k+1} \neq \hat{\boldsymbol{b}}$). Therefore, before we pick a pivot, we must check that the current Abstract Basis matches the current Abstract Vertex: $\mathbb{A}\mathbb{p}^k + \mathbb{B}^k \mathbb{s}^k - \hat{\boldsymbol{b}} = 0$ (see Eq. (18)). As with the other two cases, a failed check can be addressed by increasing the precision of the numerical algorithm. If the precision is not allowed to be increased indefinitely (i.e., it has a limit), then the procedure is not complete, since a number of problems (depending on the actual value of the precision) will not terminate with a valid result due to imprecision.

The final stage of the simplex, which corresponds to finding the support function $\max(\mathbb{v} \cdot \mathbb{p}^k)$ is trivially sound since it is the maximum of the resulting interval. Note that as stated at the beginning of this section, this is an over-approximation of the support function, given that $\mathbb{p}^k$ is an over-approximation in itself.

5.4   Vertex Enumeration

Vertex enumeration (step 9 in Algorithm 1) is an algorithm similar to simplex since it operates on the idea of visiting each vertex once in order to enumerate them.

The standard (non-interval) vertex enumeration algorithm starts by finding a base $\boldsymbol{V}^K$ which contains a number of vertices of the polyhedron. The index K is a set indicating the state of the algorithm by enumerating the rows of $\boldsymbol{A}$ that have been evaluated thus far. The process starts by pivoting over a number of different rows in $\boldsymbol{A}$ (using a simplex algorithm) and by selecting the feasible points visited, which are known to be vertices of the polyhedron. For this stage of the algorithm in the interval case, the use of a simplex as described in Sect. 5.3 ensures overall soundness. The base $\boldsymbol{V}^K$ is then iteratively expanded to $\boldsymbol{V}^{K+j}$ by exploring the jth row of $\boldsymbol{A}$ (denoted $\boldsymbol{r}^j$). The corresponding pairs $(\boldsymbol{A}^{K+j}, \boldsymbol{V}^{K+j})$ are constructed using the information from $(\boldsymbol{A}^K, \boldsymbol{V}^K)$ as follows:

Theorem 6. *Let*

$$\boldsymbol{A}^K \in \mathbb{R}^{n_K \times p} \wedge \boldsymbol{r}_i^j \in \mathbb{R}^{1 \times p} \wedge \boldsymbol{V}^K \in \mathbb{R}^{p \times m_K}.$$

where p is the dimension of the polyhedron, n_K the number of elements in the set K and m_K the number of vertices found up until stage K.

$$H_j^+ = \{\boldsymbol{x} : \boldsymbol{r}^j \boldsymbol{x} > 0\}, \quad H_j^- = \{\boldsymbol{x} : \boldsymbol{r}^j \boldsymbol{x} < 0\}, \quad H_j^0 = \{\boldsymbol{x} : \boldsymbol{r}^j \boldsymbol{x} = 0\} \quad (41)$$

be the spaces outside inside and on the jth hyperplane with respect to the polyhedron. and

$$V^{K+} = \left\{ \boldsymbol{p}^+ \in \boldsymbol{V}^K \cap H_j^+ \right\}$$
$$V^{K-} = \left\{ \boldsymbol{p}^- \in \boldsymbol{V}^K \cap H_j^- \right\}$$
$$V^{K0} = \left\{ \boldsymbol{p}^0 \in \boldsymbol{V}^K \cap H_j^0 \right\} \quad (42)$$

the existing vertex candidates lying in each of these spaces.
New vertex candidates are found as a linear combination of existing ones given a previously unused known constraint $\boldsymbol{r}^j$:

$$V^{K+j} = V^K \cup \left\{ \left(\boldsymbol{r}^j \boldsymbol{p}_k^+\right) \boldsymbol{p}_{k'}^- - \left(\boldsymbol{r}^j \boldsymbol{p}_{k'}^-\right) \boldsymbol{p}_k^+ : k \in [1 \ m_K^+] \wedge k' \in [1 \ m_K^-] \right\}. \quad (43)$$

where m_K^- and m_K^+ are the number of vertices in V^{K-} and V^{K+} respectively, $\boldsymbol{p}_k^-$ and $\boldsymbol{p}_k^+$ are points contained in the sets, and $\boldsymbol{r}^j$ is the selected row of $\boldsymbol{A}$ to be added to $\boldsymbol{A}^K$.

For the proof see [14].

Let us now consider the interval arithmetic equivalent of this theorem. Interval arithmetic ensures the soundness of the calculation

$$\mathbb{p}_{kk'} \in \boldsymbol{V}^{K+j} = \left(\mathbb{r}^j \mathbb{p}_k^+\right) \mathbb{p}_{k'}^- - \left(\mathbb{r}^j \mathbb{p}_{k'}^-\right) \mathbb{p}_k^+,$$

so all we need to ensure is the inclusions in (42).

If we expand for one of the sets, we get

$$[V^K]^+ = \left\{ \mathbb{p}^+ \in [\boldsymbol{V}^K] \cap [H_j]^+ : [H_j]^+ = \left\{ \mathbb{x} : \mathbb{r}^j \mathbb{x} > 0 \right\} \right\}$$

where the inclusion in $[H_j]^+$ becomes the concern, namely because using interval arithmetic we may find points that are either partially included (i.e., a portion of the interval, but not all of it, belongs to the set). Once again, we find that Eq. (18) ensures both the separation of the sets and the correctness of the inclusions.

Theorem 7. *Given the separation criteria in Eq. (18), the sets $[V^K]^+$, $[V^K]^-$ and $[V^K]^0$ are disjoint.*

Proof. The proof is direct from the definitions. Any point that may intersect more than one set will be marked as imprecise by (18). ☐

As with the interval simplex, the algorithm is sound but may be incomplete. Since there always exists a precision that implies a sufficiently small rounding error (given that the error decreases monotonically with increasing precision), completeness can be achieved by increasing precision at a higher processing time cost.

6   Experimental Results

The results discussed in the previous sections have been implemented in the tool Axelerator using *eigen* [17] for algebraic operations and *boost* [34] to manage intervals. Interval comparisons are implemented independently to follow our choice of ordering. The tool has been tested in a number of benchmarks (available with the tool) to determine the nature of the numerical errors. The benchmarks have been first run using unsound standard long double precision and multiple precision arithmetic with the required precision for the problem to be solved correctly (i.e., the precision demanded by our sound algorithm). The results are presented in Table 1.

Table 1. Axelerator: time performance on various benchmarks. Dimension is the number of variables in the problem; ld denotes long double precision; mp is the required precision for the algorithm using non-interval arithmetic; mpi is the sound algorithm; exact is the sound algorithm run using exact arithmetic; t.o. denotes timeout. * returns invalid data (nan)

Benchmark	Dimension	Unsound (ld)	Unsound (mp)	Sound (mpi)	Exact
Building	48	18 s	185 s	558 s	t.o.
issr10	10	2 s*	23 s	41 s	t.o.
Convoy car 3	6	0.3 s	1.3 s	3.6 s	24.6 s
Convoy car 2	3	13 ms	33 ms	73 ms	5.46 s
Parabola	4	12 ms	12 ms	47 ms	2.5 s

It can be seen from the results that the cost of using sound arithmetic is approximately 3 times that of using floating points of the same precision. The bigger cost for larger dimensional models is the requirement to use a higher precision arithmetic. This happens because the intervals grow constantly (whereas regular floating point errors often cancel themselves out resulting in a smaller overall error), and the model requires the higher precision to maintain a representative model. Accepting larger errors however can result in both too conservative results and cycling in the simplex (which results in non-termination), so we must accept this need for the algorithm to work. The cost of using an exact arithmetic simplex to evaluate an interval Tableau is combinatorial, hence for example, a 10-dimensional Tableau would require 2^{10} operations which is clearly worse than any time increase required in this paper. The alternative, which is also requiring exact arithmetic in the eigen-decomposition, can be very costly (see last column in Table 1). Thus, our algorithm offers a good tradeoff between fast unsound algorithms and slow exact ones.

7   Conclusion

We have developed a numerical multiple precision floating point interval algorithm for abstract acceleration. The results have shown that the round-of errors are relatively negligible for a large number of classes for a given precision. We have also demonstrated that the use of sound intervals comes at a relatively low processing cost of around 3x for the case of low precision systems (i.e., when the initially supplied precision suffices to ensure soundness), and a linear increase in cost with respect to precision when higher precision is required. Future work would include the use of variable precision arithmetic that would allow us to increase the precision only at the desired steps, *eg* when abstract vertices intersect.

References

1. Anderson, E., Bai, Z., Dongarra, J., Greenbaum, A., McKenney, A., Du Croz, J., Hammerling, S., Demmel, J., Bischof, C., Sorensen, D.: Lapack: a portable linear algebra library for high-performance computers. In: Proceedings of the 1990 ACM/IEEE Conference on Supercomputing, pp. 2–11. IEEE Computer Society Press (1990)
2. Bak, S., Duggirala, P.S.: Hylaa: a tool for computing simulation-equivalent reachability for linear systems. In: Proceedings of the 20th International Conference on Hybrid Systems: Computation and Control, HSCC 2017, Pittsburgh, PA, USA, 18–20 April 2017, pp. 173–178 (2017),
3. Bouissou, O., Mimram, S., Chapoutot, A.: Hyson: set-based simulation of hybrid systems. In: 2012 23rd IEEE International Symposium on Rapid System Prototyping (RSP), pp. 79–85. IEEE (2012)
4. Bradley, S., Hax, A., Magnanti, T.: Applied Mathematical Programming (1977)
5. Bustince, H., Galar, M., Bedregal, B., Kolesarova, A., Mesiar, R.: A new approach to interval-valued choquet integrals and the problem of ordering in interval-valued fuzzy set applications. IEEE Trans. Fuzzy Syst. **21**(6), 1150–1162 (2013)
6. Cattaruzza, D., Abate, A., Schrammel, P., Kroening, D.: Unbounded-time analysis of guarded LTI systems with inputs by abstract acceleration. In: Blazy, S., Jensen, T. (eds.) SAS 2015. LNCS, vol. 9291, pp. 312–331. Springer, Heidelberg (2015). doi:10.1007/978-3-662-48288-9_18
7. Chen, L., Miné, A., Cousot, P.: A sound floating-point polyhedra abstract domain. In: Ramalingam, G. (ed.) APLAS 2008. LNCS, vol. 5356, pp. 3–18. Springer, Heidelberg (2008). doi:10.1007/978-3-540-89330-1_2
8. Chen, X., Ábrahám, E., Sankaranarayanan, S.: Flow*: an analyzer for non-linear hybrid systems. In: Sharygina, N., Veith, H. (eds.) CAV 2013. LNCS, vol. 8044, pp. 258–263. Springer, Heidelberg (2013). doi:10.1007/978-3-642-39799-8_18
9. Debreu, G.: Representation of a preference ordering by a numerical function. Decis. Process. **3**, 159–165 (1954)

10. Felsner, S.: Interval orders: combinatorial structure and algorithms. Technische Universität Berlin (1992)
11. Fishburn, P.C.: Interval Orders and Interval Graphs - A Study of Partially Ordered Sets. Wiley, Hoboken (1985)
12. Fousse, L., Hanrot, G., Lefèvre, V., Pélissier, P., Zimmermann, P.: MPFR: a multiple-precision binary floating-point library with correct rounding. ACM Trans. Math. Softw. (TOMS) **33**(2), 13 (2007)
13. Frehse, G., et al.: SpaceEx: scalable verification of hybrid systems. In: Gopalakrishnan, G., Qadeer, S. (eds.) CAV 2011. LNCS, vol. 6806, pp. 379–395. Springer, Heidelberg (2011). doi:10.1007/978-3-642-22110-1_30
14. Fukuda, K., Prodon, A.: Double description method revisited. In: Deza, M., Euler, R., Manoussakis, I. (eds.) CCS 1995. LNCS, vol. 1120, pp. 91–111. Springer, Heidelberg (1996). doi:10.1007/3-540-61576-8_77
15. Gleixner, A.M., Steffy, D.E., Wolter, K.: Iterative refinement for linear programming. INFORMS J. Comput. **28**(3), 449–464 (2016)
16. Goldberg, D.: What every computer scientist should know about floating-point arithmetic. ACM Comput. Surv. (CSUR) **23**(1), 5–48 (1991)
17. Guennebaud, G., Jacob, B., et al.: Eigen v3 (2010) http://eigen.tuxfamily.org
18. Hong, Y., Pan, C.T.: A lower bound for the smallest singular value. Linear Algebra Appl. **172**, 27–32 (1992)
19. IEEE Task P754: IEEE 754–2008, Standard for Floating-Point Arithmetic, August 2008
20. Jeannet, B., Miné, A.: APRON: a library of numerical abstract domains for static analysis. In: Bouajjani, A., Maler, O. (eds.) CAV 2009. LNCS, vol. 5643, pp. 661–667. Springer, Heidelberg (2009). doi:10.1007/978-3-642-02658-4_52
21. Jeannet, B., Schrammel, P., Sankaranarayanan, S.: Abstract acceleration of general linear loops. In: POPL, pp. 529–540. ACM (2014)
22. Laub, A.J.: Matrix Analysis for Scientists and Engineers. SIAM (2005)
23. Lawson, C.L., Hanson, R.J., Kincaid, D.R., Krogh, F.T.: Basic linear algebra subprograms for Fortran usage. ACM Trans. Math. Softw. (TOMS) **5**(3), 308–323 (1979)
24. Le Lann, C., Boland, D., Constantinides, G.: The Krawczyk algorithm: rigorous bounds for linear equation solution on an FPGA. In: Koch, A., Krishnamurthy, R., McAllister, J., Woods, R., El-Ghazawi, T. (eds.) ARC 2011. LNCS, vol. 6578, pp. 287–295. Springer, Heidelberg (2011). doi:10.1007/978-3-642-19475-7_31
25. MATLAB: version 7.10.0 (R2010a). The MathWorks Inc., Natick (2010)
26. Monniaux, D.: On using floating-point computations to help an exact linear arithmetic decision procedure. In: Bouajjani, A., Maler, O. (eds.) CAV 2009. LNCS, vol. 5643, pp. 570–583. Springer, Heidelberg (2009). doi:10.1007/978-3-642-02658-4_42
27. Muller, J.M., et al.: Handbook of Floating-Point Arithmetic. Springer, Boston (2009). doi:10.1007/978-0-8176-4705-6
28. Neumaier, A., Shcherbina, O.: Safe bounds in linear and mixed-integer linear programming. Math. Program. **99**(2), 283–296 (2004)
29. de Oliveira, D.C.B., Monniaux, D.: Experiments on the feasibility of using a floating-point simplex in an SMT solver. In: PAAR@ IJCAR, pp. 19–28 (2012)
30. Pryce, J.: The forthcoming IEEE standard 1788 for interval arithmetic. In: Nehmeier, M., Wolff von Gudenberg, J., Tucker, W. (eds.) SCAN 2015. LNCS, vol. 9553, pp. 23–39. Springer, Cham (2016). doi:10.1007/978-3-319-31769-4_3
31. Revol, N., Makino, K., Berz, M.: Taylor models and floating-point arithmetic: proof that arithmetic operations are validated in COSY. J. Logic Algebraic Program. **64**(1), 135–154 (2005)

32. Rump, S.M.: Computational error bounds for multiple or nearly multiple eigenvalues. Linear Algebra Appl. **324**(1–3), 209–226 (2001)
33. Saad, Y.: Numerical Methods for Large Eigenvalue Problems, vol. 158. SIAM (1992)
34. Schäling, B.: The Boost C++ Libraries. Boris Schäling (2011)
35. Steele, J.M.: The Cauchy-Schwarz Master Class: An Introduction to the Art of Mathematical Inequalities. Cambridge University Press, Cambridge (2004)
36. Van Loan, C.F.: Matrix Computations. The Johns Hopkins University Press, Baltimore (1996)

Studying the Numerical Quality of an Industrial Computing Code: A Case Study on Code_aster

François Févotte$^{(\boxtimes)}$ (ID) and Bruno Lathuilière

Département PERICLES, EDF R&D, 7 bd Gaspard Monge, 91120 Palaiseau, France
{francois.fevotte,bruno.lathuiliere}@edf.fr

Abstract. We present in this paper a process which is suitable for the complete analysis of the numerical quality of a large industrial scientific computing code. Random rounding, using the Verrou diagnostics tool, is first used to evaluate the numerical stability, and locate the origin of errors in the source code. Once a small code part is identified as unstable, it can be isolated and studied using higher precision computations and interval arithmetic to compute guaranteed reference results. An alternative implementation of this unstable algorithm is then proposed and experimentally evaluated. Finally, error bounds are given for the proposed algorithm, and the effectiveness of the proposed corrections is assessed in the computing code.

Keywords: Floating-point · Numerical verification · Random rounding

1 Introduction

EDF is France's main electric utility. Like several other industries, its internal processes rely heavily on numerical simulations, which are performed by Scientific Computing Codes (SCC). To name only an example: numerous SCCs are used to study the safety of nuclear power plants, or optimize their production. It is therefore important that both EDF itself, but also others – like nuclear safety authorities, have confidence in the results produced by these codes. To this end, all SCCs undergo a Verification & Validation (V&V) process, during which various sources of errors are evaluated:

- modeling errors, *i.e.* differences between "real life" and the mathematical objects used to represent it;
- mathematical approximations, *i.e.* differences due to the simplification of the mathematical problem (such as discretization for example) or to their approximate resolution (for example using iterative processes);
- computation errors, due to the difference between the ideal manipulation of real numbers, and actual computations performed by program running on a CPU, which typically uses floating-point arithmetic as standardized by the IEEE-754 norm [8].

© Springer International Publishing AG 2017
A. Abate and S. Boldo (Eds.): NSV 2017, LNCS 10381, pp. 61–80, 2017.
DOI: 10.1007/978-3-319-63501-9_5

The first two sources of errors mentioned above have been studied for a long time, as they were the more dominant terms. However, continual progress in computational power over the last decades, as well as advances in numerical methods, have made it possible to dramatically increase the complexity of models, while at the same time improving their resolution (for example through refined discretizations). The impact of computing errors on results has therefore recently become of non-negligible importance, and the analysis of floating-point arithmetic is now a topic of interest for industry. However, as of today, the introduction of adequate methodologies in industrial V&V processes still largely remains to be done.

The main objective of the present paper is to describe a process which is suitable for the complete analysis of floating-point errors and numerical instabilities in a large industrial code such as code_aster.

Code_aster [1] is an open source scientific computation code dedicated to the simulation of structural mechanics and thermomechanics. It has been actively developed since 1989, mainly by the R&D division of EDF. It uses finite elements to solve models coming from the continuum mechanics theory, and can be used to perform simulations in a wide variety of physical fields such as mechanics, thermal physics, acoustics, seismology... Code_aster has a very large source code base, with more than 1 200 000 lines of code, mostly written in 3 languages: Fortran90 ($\simeq 60\%$), C ($\simeq 20\%$) and Python ($\simeq 20\%$). It also uses numerous third-party software, such as linear solvers or mesh manipulation tools. Its development team has been dedicated to code quality for a long time, and has accumulated several hundreds of test cases which are run frequently as part of the V&V process.

Despite this, the development team of code_aster has faced numerous non-reproducibilities and other errors thought to be related to floating-point arithmetic. The traditional methodology to identify and track such errors relied on the analysis of the robustness of the code to changes in its input parameters. Perturbing the mesh used in the discretization of the underlying Partial Differential Equations (PDEs) was a good way of performing such an analysis: results of the computation should be unaffected by the numbering of meshes, or almost unaffected by very small perturbations of the mesh nodes. Checking the robustness of computed results to such changes would allow to uncover errors related to numerical instabilities. The approach that we describe here is complementary: we study the robustness of the code with respect to the underlying arithmetic and perturbation of the computational process itself.

In the rest of this paper, we present a complete process allowing to study the numerical quality of code_aster, from evaluating its numerical stability (Sect. 2) and finding the origin of instabilities in the source code (Sect. 3), to fixing problems by proposing more stable algorithms (Sect. 4). The effectiveness of the proposed correction is then assessed in Sect. 5, before we make a few concluding notes in Sect. 6.

2   Checking for Numerical Instabilities with Verrou

Among the different techniques which can be used to evaluate numerical instabilities and round-off errors, the wide family of methods revolving around Monte-Carlo Arithmetic (MCA) [20] seems to be one of the most promising in industrial contexts. For example, Discrete Stochastic Arithmetic, as implemented in the CADNA library [9,11], has already been successfully used on large industrial codes [12]. However, the need for a complete instrumentation of the source code makes CADNA too costly a solution for it to be applied widely to industrial codes. Even less demanding tools such as Verificarlo [3], which only requires a re-compilation of all the source code (potentially including third-party libraries, if one wants to analyze them), are too impractical to be applied routinely as part of the V&V process of such a large code as code_aster.

In order to avoid the need for an instrumentation of the program sources or a recompilation, various tools aim at implementing numerical debugging in the form of a Dynamic Binary Analysis (DBA), *i.e.* by directly analyzing the executable binary program during its execution. For example, Craft HPC [10] is a tool performing DBA in order to detect cancellation errors, and evenmore optimize the use of single- and double-precision variables throughout the source code to balance speed and accuracy. Among DBA tools, many make the choice of leveraging the powerful DBA features of the Valgrind [13] platform. Such solutions are more advantageous since Valgrind is already used by a large number of scientific code developers to help with memory debugging, and is thus compatible with most computing codes.

FpDebug [2] is one of the earliest Valgrind-based floating-point analysis tools. It makes use of the "shadow memory" feature of Valgrind to perform a high-precision computation alongside the standard execution of the analyzed program. A comparison between high and standard precision results is performed to detect the occurrence of inaccuracies and, for each inaccuracy, to determine whether it comes from input data or from the floating-point operation itself. Apart from its very large overhead, mostly due to the use of shadow memory, the major problem preventing the use of FpDebug for industry-scale programs is the very large size of the output it produces. This problem should be tackled by Herbgrind [17], a promising tool which also uses shadow executions to detect floating-point inaccuracies, but uses advanced techniques to precisely track the origin of such errors in the source code. The Herbgrind output is therefore reduced to the set of code fragments which lead to inaccuracies, in a suitable form for later analysis with Herbie [16]. The large overhead induced by this in-depth analysis and the use of shadow memory in Valgrind—currently of the order of $\times 10$ to $\times 10\,000$ depending on the test case—makes the tool more suitable for the analysis of a single unstable test case, once the presence of numerical instabilities has already been uncovered (*cf.* Sect. 3).

2.1   Presentation of Verrou

The present work is based on Verrou [5,6], an open-source[1] floating-point arithmetic diagnostics tool developed by the R&D division of EDF. From the beginning of its development, Verrou has targeted large industrial applications by
ensuring that basic diagnostics features can always work without recompiling
the analyzed program nor having access to its source code.

Like other Valgrind-based tools, a major advantage of Verrou is its simplicity
of use. When running a program, one only needs to add a prefix to the command
line in order to instrument it:

```
valgrind --tool=verrou --rounding-mode=random PROGRAM [ARGS]
```

When called in this way, Verrou makes use of the Dynamic Binary Analysis (DBA) features of Valgrind to instrument the program (in binary form, as
it was produced by its standard industrial build process) and to replace each
floating-point instruction by a modified version which yields randomly rounded
results. Global results of the computations are thus output like in any normal
execution, except that they are affected by the cumulative effect of all randomly
rounded intermediate results. As such, Verrou implements a Random Rounding
Arithmetic (RRA), which might be seen either as a subset of MCA, or as a form
of asynchronous CESTAC method [21].

This makes it easy for Verrou to be introduced in an industrial V&V process:
as depicted in Fig. 1a, SCCs always have a non-regression test suite in which
numerous test-cases are run to produce results which are compared to references.
A tooling machinery often produces a nicely formatted synthesis of the results
in order for the developers to see at a glance whether a change introduced in
the code breaks something. Figure 1b presents how, by simply ensuring that test
cases are run within Verrou, their results can be perturbed using RRA. Such
results can then be compared as usual to references, in order to evaluate the
numerical stability of the analyzed computing code.

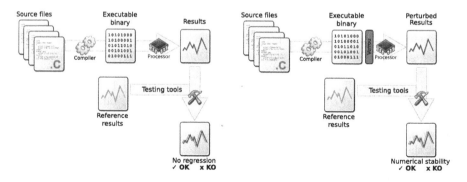

(a) Standard non-regression testing   (b) Numerical verification with Verrou

Fig. 1. Schematic view of industrial verification processes

---

[1] Project page URL: http://github.com/edf-hpc/verrou.

The overhead of Verrou is kept as low as possible by a careful implementation of the various operations in directed rounding, limiting the number of random number generations, and using fused multiply-add (FMA) instructions when the hardware supports it. Overall, the slow-down factor for one execution of a given program in Verrou with respect to native run times is usually measured between $\times 10$ and $\times 20$. The most extreme overheads that we have measured so far were $\times 8$ (for a code spending much time in I/O operations) and $\times 40$ (observed in one test-case of an extremely well-optimized code). These factors then have to be multiplied by the number of random rounding runs needed for triggering anomalies; 3–5 is usually enough.

Verrou also provides more advanced features, such as the ability to limit instrumentation to parts of the code (functions, or even source lines if the binary was compiled using the "-g" switch).

2.2   Preliminary Work

In order to check that the instrumentation process itself does not introduce errors, it is interesting to perform a preliminary study. We work here on a subset of 72 test cases, covering a wide range of features in code_aster. We took care to include in this selection some test cases known (or believed) to be unstable, and some not known to be particularly unstable. For each of these test cases, we check that:

- several standard runs of code_aster yield reproducible results;
- several runs of code_aster within Valgrind (memcheck) yield results which are both reproducible and identical to the results of a standard run;
- several runs of code_aster within Verrou in nearest mode yield results which are both reproducible and identical to the results of a standard run.

This allows for an early detection of instrumentation problems, which could otherwise invalidate the conclusions of further studies. For instance, the origin of such problems include:

introspection: when part of the code examines its own execution (*e.g.* memory consumption or elapsed times) to make choices, it is to be expected that overheads induced by the instrumentation cause differences in results;

use of 80-bit instructions: the use of 80-bit instructions coming from the x87 set results in tricky non-reproducibilities, since intermediate results can be either kept in 80-bits registers, or stored as 64-bit double-precision numbers in memory. What actually takes place in the CPU can differ between native executions, and executions within Valgrind;

use of non-default floating-point arithmetic, *e.g.* directed rounding, or specific floating-point exceptions. These might not be correctly taken into account by Valgrind/Verrou.

For code_aster, these preliminary checks allowed to uncover a minor incompatibility between the instrumentation in Verrou and the **dgemv** routine from the OpenBLAS library. Investigations are under way to determine whether this behaviour is expected and understandable (*i.e.* this situation falls into one of the three categories mentioned above), or whether it is a bug. In the latter case, this could be either a bug in Verrou, such as an incorrect handling of some specific instruction used in this routine, or a real instability in OpenBLAS.

In the meantime, this routine has been replaced (using the LD_PRELOAD mechanism) by its equivalent from the Netlib implementation of the BLAS interface. Hence, the stability problem is temporarily curbed so as to focus on the analysis of code_aster itself.

2.3 Numerical Verification Using Random Rounding

We now perform the numerical verification of code_aster using random rounding with Verrou. For the sake of brevity, although this analysis has been performed on the 72 test cases mentioned above, Table 1 only presents the results for a few test cases. Each test case is identified by its name in the first column. The following 4 columns present the status of the run, as reported by the non-regression testing tools, respectively for a run under Verrou in nearest rounding mode, and 3 runs with Verrou in random rounding mode.

We present in the last column the number of significant (decimal) digits in common between the results of the three random rounding runs. This number is defined as

$$C(x) = \log_{10} \left| \frac{\mu(x)}{\sigma(x)} \right|,$$

where, for a sample $x = (x_1, x_2, \ldots, x_N)$, we denote by $\mu(x)$ its average, and $\sigma(x)$ its standard deviation. A star (*) denotes the fact that all digits output by code_aster were identical in the different runs in random rounding (*i.e.* in such cases, we have $\sigma(x) = 0$ in the above formula, but do not know whether this is due to results being "perfectly stable", or code_aster outputting too few

Table 1. Analysis of numerical instabilities with random rounding

Test case	Status				# common digits
	nearest	rnd$_1$	rnd$_2$	rnd$_3$	$C(\text{rnd}_1, \text{rnd}_2, \text{rnd}_3)$
ssls108i	OK	OK	OK	OK	11 10
ssls108j	OK	OK	OK	OK	10 10
ssls108k	OK	OK	OK	OK	11 10
ssls108l	OK	OK	OK	OK	11 9
sdnl112a	OK	KO	KO	KO	6 6 6 * 3 0
ssnp130a	OK	OK	OK	OK	* * 10 10 10 10 9 * * * 9 9 9 9 * * 10
ssnp130b	OK	OK	OK	OK	* * 11 11 * 12 9 * * * 9 9 9 9 9 9 * *
ssnp130c	OK	OK	OK	OK	* 11 11 11 11 10 9 11 11 10 10 10 * 11
ssnp130d	OK	OK	OK	OK	* 9 * * * 10 9 9 9 9 9 9 9 * 9 * * *

digits). The column contains several numbers, as each test case performs non-regression testing on several results. For example, test case `ssls108i` outputs two results, each one of them being compared to a reference value. For the first one, the 3 random rounding runs produce values that have 11 decimal digits in common. Likewise, values produced by the 3 random runs for the second result have 10 decimal digits in common.

One (native) run of the test suite (72 test cases) takes around 10 min to complete, and each random-rounding run of the test suite with Verrou takes approximately 20 min. Therefore, the analysis presented here (one native and 3 random rounding runs) takes approximately 70 min to complete. The relatively low global overhead is explained by two factors:

- a large part of the test suite run time is spent in file-system manipulations and other I/O operations;
- the overhead of a random rounding run is relatively low, around ×10 on average between test cases.

Over the 72 test cases used in this study, 3 exhibit an unstable behaviour as shown for example by `sdnl112a` in Table 1: such tests may fail in random rounding mode and/or produce results that have very few significant digits in common between random rounding runs (3 or less).

In the rest of this paper, we focus on the further analysis of test case `sdnl112a`. Now that it has been shown to exhibit an unstable behaviour, the next logical step consists in trying to locate the origin of these instabilities within the source code, in order to correct them.

3   Locating the Origin of Numerical Errors in the Source Code

Verrou provides different ways to locate the origin of numerical errors, adapted to these different types of errors. A first technique, described in Sect. 3.1, allows the identification of functions and source code lines which produce large changes in the results when perturbed with random rounding. This is useful to locate the source of numerical errors but, in some instances, such sources of errors produce very small (and legitimate) inaccuracies, whose large impact on the final result only comes from an unstable test occurring later during program execution. In such instances, it is more appropriate to fix branching instabilities rather than the source of round-off errors. Another technique, described in Sect. 3.2, allows finding such unstable tests.

An interesting extension to the present study would consist in testing the relevance of high-overhead/high-fidelity tools such as Herbgrind, since the scope of the analysis at this stage is now reduced to one test case.

3.1   Delta-Debugging to Locate Round-Off Error Sources

A first technique relies on Verrou's ability to restrict the scope of random rounding perturbations to parts of the program: functions, and possibly source code lines if the program was compiled with the right options (like `gcc -g` for instance). Starting from a situation where perturbing the whole program produces significant errors, this feature can be used to perform a binary search (based on the Delta-Debugging (DD) algorithm [22]) that progressively reduces the scope of instrumentation in order to eventually identify unstable portions of the source code, whose perturbation produces large changes in the results [5].

Performing an analysis of test case `sdnl112a` using the Delta-Debugging technique takes approximately 2 h 20 min. Overall, the Delta-Debugging algorithm tests 86 configurations (*i.e.* subsets of functions or lines which are perturbed). A configuration is considered correct if 15 random rounding runs pass the test suite criteria. Each random rounding run take approximately 10.3 s. to run (*vs.* 3.9 s. for a nearest rounding run).

In a first stage, the search identifies one unstable function, named `mrmmvr`. In a second stage, the Delta-Debugging search refines the localization and identifies 5 unstable lines, as shown in Fig. 2.

Although it might not be obvious at first sight, function `mrmmvr` performs the product between a sparse matrix M and several vectors v_k. Unstable lines identified by the DD algorithm correspond to the dot products between each line $M[i,:]$ of the matrix and each vector $v_k[:]$. Such errors can be fixed relatively easily by introducing a compensated sum or dot product implementation. Numerous details can be found in the literature (see for example [14] or [15]), so we will not provide further details here.

```
           do 60 jvec = 1, nbvect
              do 30 k = 1, neq
                 vectmp(k)=vect(k,jvec)
   30         continue
              if (prepos) call mrconl('DIVI', lmat, 0, 'R', vectmp,1)
              xsol(1,jvec)=xsol(1,jvec)+zr(jvalms-1+1)*vectmp(1)
              do 50 ilig = 2, neq
                 kdeb=smdi(ilig-1)+1
                 kfin=smdi(ilig)-1
                 do 40 ki = kdeb, kfin
                    jcol=smhc(ki)
                    xsol(ilig,jvec)=xsol(ilig,jvec) + zr(jvalmi-1+ki) *&
                    vectmp(jcol)
                    xsol(jcol,jvec)=xsol(jcol,jvec) + zr(jvalms-1+ki) *&
                    vectmp(ilig)
   40            continue
                 xsol(ilig,jvec)=xsol(ilig,jvec) + zr(jvalms+kfin) *&
                 vectmp(ilig)
   50         continue
              if (prepos) call mrconl('DIVI', lmat, 0, 'R', xsol(1, jvec),&
                 1)
   60      continue
```

Fig. 2. Excerpt from the source code of function `mrmmvr`, which performs the product of a sparse matrix (whose non-zero coefficients are stored in array `zr`) with multiple vectors (stored in array `vect`). Vectors resulting from these products are stored in array `xsol`. Highlighted source code lines are those detected as unstable by the Delta-Debugging algorithm.

3.2 Coverage Analysis to Locate Unstable Tests

An interesting side-effect of analyzing the binary is that Verrou is largely compatible with other forms of instrumentation based on source modification or recompilation. This composability helps devising a second localization methodology, which allows finding unstable tests. The technique consists in performing a coverage analysis of the test case in nearest rounding mode, and comparing it to the same coverage analysis performed during a random rounding run. Such a coverage analysis can be conducted using standard tools, such as using the gcov utility from the gcc suite. An example output of coverage analysis is presented in the left part of Fig. 3: the gcov tool produces annotated source files, where each line is prefixed by the number of times it was executed during the run. Dashes (-) indicate lines which do not contain executable code, and hashes (#) mark lines which were never executed.

The right part of Fig. 3 presents results of a coverage analysis performed in the same conditions, except that the program was perturbed with random rounding using Verrou. Lines highlighted in the figure are those for which the coverage count is different between the native run and the random rounding run. This identifies unstable tests, which led to different branches being taken.

This technique is much faster than the Delta-Debugging method presented above, since it only needs a few runs of the program: one standard run in nearest rounding mode, and as few random rounding runs as necessary to trigger instabilities (ideally only one, as it is the case here). A small additional overhead is due to the gcov instrumentation but, overall, the analysis of unstable tests in case sdnl112a takes less than a minute to complete.

Three unstable tests were found this way in code_aster, including the function illustrated in Fig. 3, on which we will focus in the rest of this paper. A quick inspection shows that the incriminated function aims at computing

$$f(a, b) = \begin{vmatrix} a & \text{if } a = b, \\ \frac{b-a}{\log(b)-\log(a)} & \text{otherwise,} \end{vmatrix} \tag{1}$$

which is a continuous function in real arithmetic, but whose current implementation in Fortran exhibits (not too unsurprisingly) unstable behavior in floating-point arithmetic. Our next step should then be to transform this formula into another expression, more stable when evaluated in floating-point arithmetic. Since the implementation presented in Fig. 3 uses the IEEE-754 *binary64* [8] format for all relevant variables (declared using real(kind=8) in Fortran), we will focus on this precision. The rest of this paper will therefore consistently use double-precision floating-point arithmetic, and define the relative rounding error as $\mathbf{u} = 2^{-53}$.

```
120:subroutine fun1(area, a1, a2, n)        120:subroutine fun1(area, a1,
  -:       implicit none                       -:       implicit none
  -:       integer :: n                        -:       integer :: n
  -:       real(kind=8) :: area, a1, a2        -:       real(kind=8) :: area,
120:       if (a1 .eq. a2) then              120:       if (a1 .eq. a2) then
 13:           area = a1                        4:           area = a1
  -:       else                                -:       else
107:           if (n .lt. 2) then            116:           if (n .lt. 2) then
107:               area = (a2-a1) / (log(a2)-log(a1))   116:               area = (a2-a1...
###:           else if (n .eq.2) then        ###:           else if (n .eq.2)...
###:               area = sqrt (a1*a2)       ###:               area = sqrt (...
  -:           else                            -:           else
###:                                          ###:               ! ...
  -:               endif                        -:               endif
  -:       endif                               -:       endif
120:end subroutine                           120:end subroutine
```

Fig. 3. Instability detection using code coverage diagnostic tools: results of a standard coverage diagnostic (left), compared to a coverage diagnostic perturbed with random rounding using Verrou (right). Highlighted source code lines are those for which the count of occurrences is different in both executions.

4   Fixing Floating-Point Instabilities

Instabilities such as the one uncovered here can quickly be studied by developing a small stand-alone application performing only the calculation of $f(a, b)$. Since the scope of the analysis is now reduced to a single code fragment, the field of applicable tools considerably widens. For example, one approach could consist in performing a static analysis of the code. However, all we interested in here is fixing the expression, which exactly what the Herbie tool [16] was designed to do. Herbie aims at providing more accurate replacements for expressions which are inaccurately evaluated in floating-point arithmetic. It does so by evaluating the input expression on a sample of all parameters in order to assess its accuracy by comparison between standard precision floating-point arithmetic

---

Algorithm 1. Floating-point implementation of the proposed formula

---

Data: a, b

Result: $p \simeq f(a, b)$

1   $c \leftarrow b \oslash a$;

2   $n \leftarrow c \ominus 1$;

3   **if** $|n| \leq 5\,\mathrm{u}$ **then**

4 | $p \leftarrow a$;

5   **else**

6 | $l \leftarrow \mathrm{round}(\log(c))$;

7 | $f \leftarrow n \oslash l$;

8 | $p \leftarrow a \otimes f$;

9   **end**

---

and higher-precision arithmetic. Multiple transformations are then tested on the input expression in order to generate replacements, which are in turn evaluated to check whether they are more accurate than the initial one. Herbie tries by default to generate an expression that maximizes the average floating-point accuracy over the whole set of samples.

Unfortunately, in our case, expression (1) is very accurate almost everywhere in the space of parameters. The only inaccuracies occur when a and b are very close, which leads to a catastrophic cancellation between the logarithms in the denominator. Even increasing the number of points sampled by Herbie (100 000 points instead of the default 256), the subset of values for which a is close enough to b to cause error is not sampled. Therefore, even if we tell Herbie to optimize the worst case accuracy, the error is underestimated and no useful replacement is proposed. In [16], Herbie authors mention the need for a sampling of millions of points in order to correctly evaluate the worst-case accuracy of expressions with more than one argument.

4.1 Experimental Analysis of the Instability

Therefore, we revert to a by-hand, experimental analysis of expression (1). Extracting the value used when running the test case, one can let b vary in a small floating-point interval around a, for example of radius 600 **u**, and study the errors made when computing $f(a, b)$ using an implementation similar to the one used in code_aster. In our case, we take

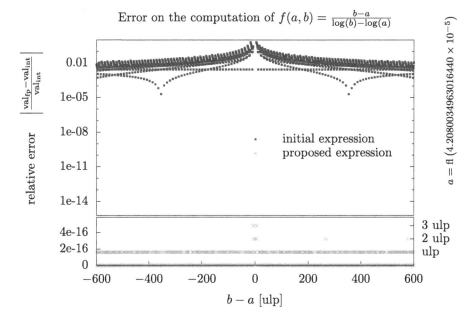

Fig. 4. Relative errors on $f(a, b)$, as computed in floating-point arithmetic using the initial implementation found in code_aster, and the corrected implementation proposed in this work (Color figure online)

$$a = 4.2080034963016440 \times 10^{-5} \quad \text{and} \quad b \in [a\,(1 - 600\,\mathbf{u}), a\,(1 + 600\,\mathbf{u})]\,.$$

One can choose any language to perform such an analysis, as the underlying floating-point arithmetic will always be the same. For the present study, we chose to use Julia, which has the advantage of proposing an easy-to-use interval arithmetics library: `ValidatedNumerics` [18]. This library makes it very easy to compute precise values of $f(a, b)$, to be used as reference when evaluating errors produced by the tested implementation. More precisely, reference results in this study have been produced using an interval arithmetic based on an underlying 112-bit floating-point arithmetic. We can check *a posteriori* that both extremities of the resulting interval are rounded to the same double-precision floating-point value, which ensures that the 112-bit precision is enough to compute an accurate approximation of the real result. This value is then used as a reference to compute the relative error of the floating-point evaluation of $f(a, b)$.

As illustrated by the red square markers in Fig. 4, the initial implementation in code_aster produces very large relative errors, sometimes higher than 60%. With such an implementation, evaluating $f(a, b)$ when b is very close to a (a few ulps) even produces infinite or NaN values.

4.2   Proposed Solution

In order to devise an alternative formulation of expression (1), equivalent in terms of real calculations but more stable with floating-point arithmetic, we need to make sure to avoid any catastrophic cancellation in the denominator. We therefore propose in this work to use the following re-definition of the function:

$$f(a, b) = \begin{vmatrix} a & \text{if } a = b, \\ a\,\dfrac{\frac{b}{a} - 1}{\log(\frac{b}{a})} & \text{otherwise.} \end{vmatrix} \tag{2}$$

Furthermore, in order to evaluate this expression using a binary floating-point arithmetic, we propose to implement it using Algorithm 1. In this algorithm, we denote by $\oplus$, $\ominus$, $\otimes$ and $\oslash$ the rounded-to-nearest floating-point versions of the basic operations. Notice that the test in Algorithm 1 has been enlarged, so that future analyses using techniques like the one described in Sect. 3 are less likely to detect a (now hopefully fixed) unstable test.

The quality of this algorithm can be evaluated using the methodology presented in the previous section. Results shown by the blue x-shaped markers in Fig. 4 clearly illustrate the improvement brought by the use of the proposed algorithm: relative errors drop from the $[10^{-5}, 10^{-1}]$ range, down to 3 ulps.

4.3   Proof

In an industrial context, the previous study would probably be enough to validate the proposed formula: most engineers would accept such experimental results are a sufficient "guarantee" that the proposed expression is correct.

Nevertheless, for the sake of completeness, we present here a mathematical proof that the proposed formula actually provides good accuracy in all cases.

Even if we depart from the pragmatic, industrial approach, such a proof will at least have a pedagogical interest, in that it gives a better understanding of why the proposed correction improves overall accuracy.

Theorem 1. *Let a and b be two floating point numbers. Then, assuming that no denormalized numbers appear during calculations, the operations described in Algorithm 1 produce a result close to $f(a, b)$, with a relative error bounded in the first order by 10 ulps.*

We assume in this proof that no overflow occurs. If we define

$$x = \frac{b}{a},$$

then we have

$$c = x\,(1 + \varepsilon_c), \tag{3}$$

where ε_c is a relative error smaller than machine precision: $|\varepsilon_c| \leq \mathbf{u}$.

In the following, we will adhere to the convention that all relative round-off errors are denoted by ε_v, where v is the name of the variable storing the result of the operation, as defined in Algorithm 1. The proof is presented in its entirety in Appendix A, and we only give a sketch of it here. We start by defining two sub-cases, corresponding to the branches of the test.

Case 1: a almost equal to b. This case corresponds to lines 3–4 in Algorithm 1. The full proof for this case is presented in Appendix A.1. It relies on the fact that, since $1 - x$ is the beginning of the Taylor development of $\log(x)$ in 1, the approximation

$$\frac{x - 1}{\log(x)} \simeq 1$$

is accurate when $x \simeq 1$.

Case 2: a "far from" b. This case corresponds to lines 5–8 in Algorithm 1. Starting from (3) and following the next statements in the algorithm, we have

$$n = (c - 1)\,(1 + \varepsilon_n), \tag{4}$$

$$l = \log(c)\,(1 + \varepsilon_l), \tag{5}$$

$$
\begin{aligned}
f &= \frac{n}{l}\,(1 + \varepsilon_f) \\
&= \frac{c - 1}{\log(c)}\,\frac{(1 + \varepsilon_n)(1 + \varepsilon_f)}{1 + \varepsilon_l},
\end{aligned} \tag{6}
$$

$$
\begin{aligned}
p &= a\,f\,(1 + \varepsilon_p) \\
&= a\,\frac{c - 1}{\log(c)}\,\frac{(1 + \varepsilon_n)\,(1 + \varepsilon_f)\,(1 + \varepsilon_p)}{1 + \varepsilon_l} \\
&= a\,\underbrace{\frac{x - 1}{\log(x)}\,\frac{c - 1}{x - 1}\,\frac{\log(x)}{\log(c)}}_{E_1}\,\underbrace{\frac{(1 + \varepsilon_n)\,(1 + \varepsilon_f)\,(1 + \varepsilon_p)}{1 + \varepsilon_l}}_{E_2}.
\end{aligned} \tag{7}
$$

We obtain in (7) that p is an approximation of the desired quantity, with a relative error given by $e = E_1 E_2 - 1$. While it is clear that E_2 is bounded and close to unity, a more thorough analysis of E_1 needs to be performed.

Indeed, when x and c are close to 1, all four terms appearing in E_1 are small, and it is not clear that E_1 can be bounded. We will thus define two sub-cases: $x \in \left[\frac{1}{2}, 2\right]$ and $x \notin \left[\frac{1}{2}, 2\right]$.

Case 2a: $x \notin \left[\frac{1}{2}, 2\right]$. This case is rather straightforward, since all terms are far enough from 0 for relative errors to stay bounded. Appendix A.2 presents the proof for this case, partly automatized with the Gappa proof assistant [4].

Case 2b: $x \in \left[\frac{1}{2}, 2\right]$. This case is maybe the most interesting one, as it explains why the proposed expression is more stable than the initial one. The idea here is that, since $1 - x$ is the beginning of the Taylor development of $\log(x)$ in 1, the function $\frac{x-1}{\log(x)}$ can not get too close to 0 in the considered interval. Moreover, its derivative can be bounded, so that the small error between x and c can not have too catastrophic consequences.

5   Checking the Effectiveness of Corrections

We can finally re-assess the numerical stability of code_aster in order to check the effectiveness of the corrections made so far.

Before using Verrou and following the protocol of Sect. 2, an important question which arises at this stage is the validity of Random Rounding Arithmetic to assess compensated algorithms such as the ones introduced to fix the problem detected in Sect. 3.1. Indeed, such algorithms were designed to work in nearest rounding mode, and could very well be incompatible with directed or random rounding. Pioneering work has been performed on this topic in [7], which shows that compensated summations and dot products will indeed work with random rounding. However, a broader study of various kinds of algorithms still needs to be performed.

Table 2 presents the results of a re-assessment of the numerical stability of test-case sdnl112a. The first line in this table comes from the initial tests presented in Table 1; the second line corresponds to the same test performed on the version of code_aster in which the instabilities uncovered in Sect. 3 were fixed.

Table 2. Analysis of numerical instabilities of test-case sdnl112a

Version	Status				# common digits
	Nearest	rnd$_1$	rnd$_2$	rnd$_3$	$C(\mathrm{rnd}_1, \mathrm{rnd}_2, \mathrm{rnd}_3)$
Before correction	OK	KO	KO	KO	6 6 6 * 3 0
After correction	OK	KO	OK	OK	9 10 8 * 5 0

We can observe that two random rounding runs now pass, and the test stability has been improved by 2 to 4 decimal digits depending on the result. The

6th result has no digit in common between random-rounding runs because it is expected to be close to 0 (and the test suite uses an absolute error to validate it, so this result is not alarming). However, the corrected version still fails the test in one random rounding run. Investigations show that this is because of the 5th result, which is not surprising since the numerical stability of this result is still relatively low, with only 5 decimal digits in common between random rounding runs. This means that some work still needs to be done in order to correct inaccuracies in this test case.

6   Conclusion and Perspectives

We have presented in this paper a complete workflow for the analysis and improvement of the numerical quality of a large industrial code, as exemplified by code_aster. An important conclusion to get from this work is that such an analysis, which would probably have been out of reach a few years ago, is now feasible. This paves the way for tighter integration of numerical verification tools within industrial Verification and Validation processes.

This work also illustrates the wide variety of techniques which can be used to perform such an analysis, and the complementarity between them:

- Random Rounding Arithmetic (RRA), as implemented in Verrou, has successfully helped to bring out the numerical instabilities in code_aster, and to locate their origin in the source code;
- compensated algorithms have allowed increasing the accuracy of large dot products in the code;
- higher precision computations (whose correctness can be guaranteed ny Interval Arithmetic) have allowed to experimentally analyze an inaccurate expression and check the validity of the proposed reformulation;
- a mathematical proof has confirmed this validity over the whole range of arguments, while giving bounds on the produced error;
- RRA can again be used to assess the effectiveness of the corrections applied to code_aster.

Nevertheless, more work still needs to be carried out on such topics. Several sources of errors have been detected in the study, but we further studied and proposed corrections for only two of them. A straightforward extension would be to try and correct other errors to further improve the overall stability of code_aster and make all its test cases reproducible and portable across architectures. Also, steps involving the precise localization of errors and the proposition of corrections could be further streamlined, either in Verrou or in tools like Herbgrind (localization) and Herbie (correction).

A   Complete Proof

A.1   Case 1: a Almost Equal to b

We treat in a first step the case where the condition in the "if" statement at line 3 of Algorithm 1 applies. In this case, a and b are close enough to one another for Sterbenz lemma [19] to hold, which means that no additional error is made when computing n:

$$n = c - 1 = x\,(1 + \varepsilon_c) - 1.$$

The condition tested at the beginning of Algorithm 1 therefore implies that:

$$\frac{1 - 5\,\mathbf{u}}{1 + \mathbf{u}} \le x \le \frac{1 + 5\,\mathbf{u}}{1 - \mathbf{u}},$$

and

$$\frac{-6\,\mathbf{u}}{1 + \mathbf{u}} \le x - 1 \le \frac{6\,\mathbf{u}}{1 - \mathbf{u}}. \tag{8}$$

The algorithm returns a in this case, instead of the exact value

$$f(a, b) = a\,\frac{x - 1}{\log(x)},$$

so that the relative error is given by:

$$
\begin{aligned}
e_0 &= \frac{a - f(a, b)}{f(a, b)} \\
&= \frac{\log(x)}{x - 1} - 1 \\
&= \frac{\log(1 + \epsilon)}{\epsilon} - 1 \qquad\qquad \text{(where } \epsilon = x - 1\text{)} \\
&= \frac{1}{\epsilon}\left(\sum_{n=0}^{\infty} \frac{(-1)^n\,\epsilon^{n+1}}{n + 1} \right) - 1 \qquad \text{(Taylor expansion of the log function)} \\
&= \sum_{n=1}^{\infty} \frac{(-1)^n\,\epsilon^n}{n + 1}. \tag{9}
\end{aligned}
$$

Assuming $\epsilon \ge 0$, we have

$$\forall n \in \mathbb{N}, \qquad \frac{\epsilon^n}{n + 1} > \frac{\epsilon^{n+1}}{n + 2},$$

so that grouping terms in pairs in (9) yields

$$e_0 = -\sum_{k=1}^{\infty}\left[\frac{\epsilon^{2k-1}}{2k} - \frac{\epsilon^{2k}}{2k + 1} \right] \le 0$$

and

$$e_0 = -\frac{\epsilon}{2} + \sum_{k=1}^{\infty}\left[\frac{\epsilon^{2k}}{2k + 1} - \frac{\epsilon^{2k+1}}{2k + 2} \right] \ge -\frac{\epsilon}{2}.$$

The case where $\epsilon < 0$ is treated similarly, so that we get

$$|e_0| \le \frac{|\epsilon|}{2} \le \frac{3\,\mathbf{u}}{1-\mathbf{u}},$$

where we injected (8) in the last inequality. This last result shows that in this case, the relative error is bound by 3 ulps in the first order.

A.2   Case 2a: $x \notin \left[\frac{1}{2}, 2\right]$

We assume in this case that $x \notin \left[\frac{1}{2}, 2\right]$, and will focus on the sub-case where $x > 2$ (the other subcase, $x < \frac{1}{2}$, can be handled in a similar way).

Starting from (3), and knowing that the logarithm is a monotonically increasing function, we have:

$$\log(c) = \log(x\,(1 + \varepsilon_c)) = \log(x) + \log(1 + \varepsilon_c),$$
$$\Longrightarrow |\log(c) - \log(x)| \le \log(1 + \mathbf{u}) \le \mathbf{u},$$

where the last inequality was obtained by noting that the logarithm is convex, and its derivative in 1 is 1. A rather simple Gappa script, presented in Fig. 5 can prove the rest. In this script, all capital letters are ideal, real values corresponding to the approximations computed in Algorithm 1 and represented by lower-case letters. We denote $\mathbf{LX} = \log(x)$, and $\mathbf{LE} = \log(c) - \log(x)$. The bound on $\mathbf{LE}$ used as hypothesis comes from the simple computation above, the bound on $\mathbf{LX}$ are those of the logarithm over the range of double-precision floating-point numbers. Other bounds come from double-precision floating-point limits.

Gappa can prove that the relative error produced by Algorithm 1 in this case is bounded by approximately 8.9×10^{-16}, which is compatible with the bounds stated in Theorem 1. It should be noted however that Gappa can't validate this script for too small values of a, probably denoting a problem with denormalized values.

A.3   Case 2b: $x \in \left[\frac{1}{2}, 2\right]$

We finally study here the case when a and b are close to one another: $x \in \left[\frac{1}{2}, 2\right]$. Let us define

$$g(x) = \frac{\log(x)}{x - 1},$$

so that, recalling the expression of E_1 from (7),

$$E_1 = \frac{g(x)}{g(c)} = \frac{g(x)}{g(x + x\,\varepsilon_c)}.$$

```
# a and b are double-precision floating-point values
@rnd = float<ieee_64, ne>;
a = rnd(A);
b = rnd(B);

# Real computation (log(X) = LX)
X = b / a;
F = (X - 1) / (LX + 0);
P = a * F;

# FP computation    (log(c) = LX + LE)
c = rnd(X);
n rnd= c - 1;
l rnd= LX + LE;
f rnd= n / l;
p rnd= a * f;

{
  # Hypotheses
  ( a     in [1b-1000, 1.8e308]   # upper bound coming from
  /\ X    in [2,        1.8e308]   # binary64 limits
  /\ LX   in [0.5,      710]
  /\ |LE| <= 1b-53)

  # Conclusion
  -> p -/ P in ?
}
```

```
Results:
  p -/ P in [-1152921504606846483b-110 {-8.88178e-16, -2^(-50)},
             1152921504606846483b-110 { 8.88178e-16,  2^(-50)}]
```

Fig. 5. Gappa script used to prove case 2a

We have:

$$|g(x + x\,\varepsilon_c) - g(x)| \leq x\,|\varepsilon_c| \sup_{y \in [x, x + x\,\varepsilon_c]} |g'(y)|$$

$$\leq x\,|\varepsilon_c| \sup_{y \in [\frac{1-u}{2}, 2+2u]} |g'(y)|$$

$$\leq 0.6\,|\varepsilon_c|,$$

where the last inequality was obtained by noticing that

$$\forall y \in \left[\frac{1-u}{2}, 2+2u\right], \quad g'(y) \in [-0.3, -0.1],$$

as shown by a simple interval analysis. A similar interval analysis shows that

$$\forall y \in \left[\frac{1}{2}, 2\right], \quad g(y) \geq \frac{1}{2},$$

so that

$$\left|\frac{g(x + x\,\varepsilon_c) - g(x)}{g(x)}\right| \leq 1.2\,|\varepsilon_c|,$$

and thus, recalling the expression of E_1 from (7),

$$\frac{1}{1 + 1.2\,|\varepsilon_{\rm c}|} \leq E_1 \leq \frac{1}{1 - 1.2\,|\varepsilon_{\rm c}|}.$$

Putting all previous results together, we therefore have

$$\frac{(1 - \mathbf{u})^3}{(1 + 1.2\,\mathbf{u})\,(1 + \mathbf{u})} \leq 1 + e \leq \frac{(1 + \mathbf{u})^3}{(1 - 1.2\,\mathbf{u})\,(1 - \mathbf{u})},$$

which proves that, in the first order, the relative error in this case is bounded by 6 ulps. It is interesting to note here that, depending on the specific floating-point implementation of the logarithm, l might not be correctly rounded and error term ε_l might be bounded by several ulps. Should this happen, the relative error on the result of Algorithm 1 would be higher, but still bounded.

References

1. Code_Aster: Structures and thermomechanics analysis for studies and research. http://www.code-aster.org/
2. Benz, F., Hildebrandt, A., Hack, S.: A dynamic program analysis to find floating-point accuracy problems. In: 33rd ACM SIGPLAN Conference on Programming Language Design and Implementation (PLDI), pp. 453–462. ACM, New York, June 2012
3. Denis, C., de Oliveira Castro, P., Petit, E.: Verificarlo: checking floating point accuracy through Monte Carlo Arithmetic. In: 23rd IEEE International Symposium on Computer Arithmetic (ARITH 2016) (2016)
4. de Dinechin, F., Lauter, C., Melquiond, G.: Certifying the floating-point implementation of an elementary function using Gappa. IEEE Trans. Comput. **60**(2), 242–253 (2011)
5. Févotte, F., Lathuilière, B.: VERROU: Assessing Floating-Point Accuracy Without Recompiling, October 2016. https://hal.archives-ouvertes.fr/hal-01383417
6. Févotte, F., Lathuilière, B.: VERROU: a CESTAC evaluation without recompilation. In: International Symposium on Scientific Computing, Computer Arithmetics and Verified Numerics (SCAN), Uppsala, Sweden, September 2016
7. Graillat, S., Jézéquel, F., Picot, R.: Numerical Validation of Compensated Algorithms with Stochastic Arithmetic, September 2016. https://hal.archives-ouvertes. fr/hal-01367769
8. IEEE Standard for Floating-Point Arithmetic. IEEE Std 754–2008, pp. 1–70 (2008)
9. Jézéquel, F., Chesneaux, J.M., Lamotte, J.L.: A new version of the CADNA library for estimating round-off error propagation in Fortran programs. Comput. Phys. Commun. **181**(11), 1927–1928 (2010)
10. Lam, M.O., Hollingsworth, J.K., Stewart, G.: Dynamic floating-point cancellation detection. Parallel Comput. **39**(3), 146–155 (2013)
11. Lamotte, J.L., Chesneaux, J.M., Jézéquel, F.: CADNA_C: a version of CADNA for use with C or C++ programs. Comput. Phys. Commun. **181**(11), 1925–1926 (2010)
12. Montan, S.: Sur la validation numérique des codes de calcul industriels. Ph.D. thesis, Université Pierre et Marie Curie (Paris 6), France (2013). (in French)

13. Nethercote, N., Seward, J.: Valgrind: a framework for heavyweight dynamic binary instrumentation. In: ACM SIGPLAN 2007 Conference on Programming Language Design and Implementation (PLDI) (2007)
14. Neumaier, A.: Rundungsfehleranalyse einiger verfahren zur summation endlicher summen. ZAMM (Zeitschrift für Angewandte Mathematik und Mechanik) **54**, 39–51 (1974)
15. Ogita, T., Rump, S.M., Oishi, S.: Accurate sum and dot product. SIAM J. Sci. Comput. **26**, 1955–1988 (2005)
16. Panchekha, P., Sanchez-Stern, A., Wilcox, J.R., Tatlock, Z.: Automatically improving accuracy for floating point expressions. In: ACM SIGPLAN Conference on Programming Language Design and Implementation (PLDI 2015), Portland, Oregon, USA, June 2015
17. Sanchez-Stern, A., Panchekha, P., Lerner, S., Tatlock, Z.: Finding root causes of floating point error with herbgrind, arXiv:1705.10416v1 [cs.PL]
18. Sanders, D.P., Benet, L., Kryukov, N.: The julia package `ValidatedNumerics.jl` and its application to the rigorous characterization of open billiard models. In: International Symposium on Scientific Computing, Computer Arithmetics and Verified Numerics (SCAN), Uppsala, Sweden, September 2016
19. Sterbenz, P.H.: Floating Point Computation. Prentice-Hall, Englewood Cliffs (1974)
20. Stott Parker, D.: Monte Carlo arithmetic: exploiting randomness in floating-point arithmetic. Technical report CSD-970002, University of California, Los Angeles (1997)
21. Vignes, J.: A stochastic arithmetic for reliable scientific computation. Math. Comput. Simul. **35**, 233–261 (1993)
22. Zeller, A.: Why Programs Fail, 2nd edn. Morgan Kaufmann, Boston (2009)

Analysis and Verification of Continuous and Hybrid Models

Challenges and Tool Implementation of Hybrid Rapidly-Exploring Random Trees

Stanley Bak[1], Sergiy Bogomolov[2], Thomas A. Henzinger[3],
and Aviral Kumar[4(✉)]

[1] Air Force Research Laboratory, Dayton, OH, USA
[2] Australian National Unviersity, Canberra, Australia
[3] IST Austria, Klosterneuberg, Austria
[4] Indian Institute of Technology Bombay, Mumbai, India
aviralkumar2907@gmail.com

Abstract. A Rapidly-exploring Random Tree (RRT) is an algorithm which can search a non-convex region of space by incrementally building a space-filling tree. The tree is constructed from random points drawn from system's state space and is biased to grow towards large unexplored areas in the system. RRT can provide better coverage of a system's possible behaviors compared with random simulations, but is more lightweight than full reachability analysis. In this paper, we explore some of the design decisions encountered while implementing a hybrid extension of the RRT algorithm, which have not been elaborated on before. In particular, we focus on handling non-determinism, which arises due to discrete transitions. We introduce the notion of important points to account for this phenomena. We showcase our ideas using heater and navigation benchmarks.

1 Introduction

Hybrid automata are mathematical models that combine discrete and continuous dynamics. This formalism can be used to analyze many real word systems. Hybrid automata analysis and particularly reachability analysis are computationally expensive and might be even intractable for large systems. Non-deterministic behavior, e.g. uncertain inputs, make analysis even more challenging [2,5,7,12]. Simulation based techniques [6] belong to a promising class of techniques to automatically detect system bugs. At the same time, these methods cannot provide any mathematical guarantees on the system safety.

Rapidly-exploring random trees (RRTs) [8,13] have been developed to address this problem. RRTs were originally proposed in the motion planning community in order to provide a fast and efficient way of to explore the search space towards given goal states. Bhatia and Frazzoli [4] and Esposito et al. [10] explored the application of RRTs for hybrid automata to provide an efficient way

---

DISTRIBUTION A. Approved for public release; Distribution unlimited. (Approval AFRL PA #88ABW-2016-4898, 30 SEP 2016).

A. Abate and S. Boldo (Eds.): NSV 2017, LNCS 10381, pp. 83–89, 2017.
DOI: 10.1007/978-3-319-63501-9_6

to generate a system simulations which provide some coverage guarantees. Plaku et al. [14] used motion planning techniques for falsification of hybrid automata.

In this paper, we discuss our experience with RRTs and particularly its adaptation to hybrid automata. We note that handling of system non-determinism poses a special challenge. For this purpose, we introduce a notion of *important points*, where an important point refers to a system state where either invariant is violated or a transition guard becomes enabled or disabled. Our algorithm uses sets of important points to find a sweet-spot between simulation time and state space coverage.

2   Preliminaries

In this paper, we consider systems modelled in terms of hybrid automata [1].

Definition 1. *A hybrid automaton is a tuple*

$$H = (S, Inv, E, G, J, U, f, I, F),$$

where

- *Q is a discrete and finite set, called modes*
- *X maps each mode to corresponding continuous state space, i.e. $q \to X_q$, where $X_q \in \mathbb{R}^{dim(X_q)}$ is the continuous state space associated with $q \in Q$*
- *$S = Q \times X$ is the Cartesian product of discrete and continuous state space*
- *Inv maps each mode to the corresponding continuous invariant, i.e. $q \xrightarrow{Inv} Inv_q$ where $Inv_q \subseteq X_q$ represents domain of the continuous variables associated with $q \in Q$*
- *$E \subseteq Q \times Q$ is the set of discrete transitions between modes*
- *G maps discrete transitions to guard conditions, i.e., $(q_i, q_j) \xrightarrow{G} G_{(q_i,q_j)}$, where $G_{(q_i,q_j)} \subseteq X_{q_i}$ is the guard condition associated with $(q_i, q_j) \in E$*
- *J maps discrete transitions to reset functions, i.e., $(q_i, q_j) \xrightarrow{J} J_{(q_i,q_j)}$ where $J_{(q_i,q_j)} : G_{(q_i,q_j)} \to X_{q_j}$ is the reset function associated with $(q_i, q_j) \in E$*
- *U maps each mode to the corresponding set of control input signals, $q \xrightarrow{U} U_q$ where $q \in Q$ and $U_q \subseteq \mathbb{R}^{dim(U_q)}$*
- *f maps each mode to the function that describes the associated continuous dynamics $q \xrightarrow{f} f_q$, where $f_q : X_q \times U_q \to \dot{X}_q$*

In the following, we briefly recall an algorithm to compute RRTs [9,13] (see Algorithm 1 for more details) for purely continuous systems. The algorithm incrementally constructs a tree of feasible trajectories. A RRT is represented by a graph $G = (V, E)$, where the set V consists of the end points of feasible trajectories and $E(v_i, v_j)$ represents the trajectory followed, and is labelled with $u \in U$, i.e. the control signal needed to reach v_j from v_i, within a time interval of the length T.

Initially, the RRT contains a single mode x_{init}. A random point $x_{rand} \in X$ is generated in each iteration (GENERATE-RANDOM), and the nearest neighbour $x_{near} \in V$ to x_{rand} is found in the tree where distance is defined by some distance metric ρ (NEAREST-NEIGHBOUR). Now, a new candidate to be added to the tree, x_{new} is found by applying control signal u for some time horizon T. The chosen control signal u minimizes the distance between x_{rand} and x_{new} (MIN-CONTROL-SIGNAL and EXTEND) The above mentioned steps are repeated until either we reach a ε neighbourhood of x_{target} or exceed number of iterations K_{max}.

3 RRT for Hybrid Automata

In this section, we discuss necessary changes to Algorithm 1 to account for mixed discrete-continuous nature of hybrid automata. We modify the procedure GENERATE-RANDOM to reflect the fact that, in the new setting, the state space consists of both discrete and continuous states. Therefore, in order to select a random point, we randomly select (1) a discrete mode $q \in Q$ and (2) a continuous point which satisfies the invariant Inv_q. In order to define a distance measure in the hybrid state space in the NEAREST-NEIGHBOUR procedure, we follow the approach suggested by Bhatia and Frazzoli [4]. In particular, the distance between two nodes $z_1 = (q, x_1)$ and $z_2 = (q, x_2)$ lying in the same discrete mode is given by $D(z_1, z_2) = d(x_1, x_2)$ where $d(.,.)$ is a standard L_1, L_∞ or Euclidean measure. For two states which belong to different discrete modes, distance is given by a tuple

$$D(z_1, z_2) = (\delta(q_1, q_2), \min_{\forall q \in q_{next}} d(x_1, G(q_1, q))),$$

where $\delta(q_1, q_2)$ denotes the number of nodes on the shortest path from mode q_1 to mode q_2 in graph induced by the discrete structure of the hybrid automaton H and

Procedure RRT($x_{init}, x_{target}, \varepsilon$)
$V = x_{init}, E \leftarrow \emptyset, k = 1, x_{new} = +\infty$;
while $k \leq K_{max} \wedge d(x_{new}, x_{target}) > \varepsilon$ **do**
  $\quad x_{rand}$ = GENERATE-RANDOM();
  $\quad x_{near}$ = NEAREST-NEIGHBOUR(x_{rand}, V, ρ);
  $\quad u_{min}$ = MIN-CONTROL-SIGNAL(x_{rand}, x_{near});
  $\quad x_{new}$ = EXTEND(x_{near}, u_{min});
  $\quad V \leftarrow V \cup x_{new}$;
  $\quad E \leftarrow E \cup (x_{new}, x_{near}, u_{min})$;
  $\quad k = k + 1$;
end

Algorithm 1: Algorithm to construct a RRT. The algorithm starts with the single mode x_{init} and grows the tree uniformly until x_{target} or a threshold on number of iterations K_{max} has been reached. The tuple (V, E) stores the current state of the RRT. The used distance measure is referred to as ρ.

$$q_{next} = \{q \in Q | (\delta(q, q_2) < \delta(q_1, q_2)) \wedge E(q_1, q)\}.$$

Geometrically speaking, q_{next} is the set of nodes which are at one edge distance from q_1 and which reduce the path length to q_2 from q_1 by one discrete jump. The procedure, MIN-CONTROL-SIGNAL finds the control input $u \in \mathcal{U}$ which minimizes the distance between x_{rand} and a state reachable from x_{near} within the time frame T. Now, we observe that due to possible *non-determinism* in the hybrid automaton behavior, the state reachable within the time frame T is not uniquely defined. In the next section, we discuss this issue in more details.

4   Non-determinism Handling

We recall that hybrid automata exhibit non-determinism due to discrete mode switches. In particular, for the discrete modes q and q', the mode switch is enabled as long as the system is in the set $Inv_q \cap G(q, q') \cap Inv_{q'}$. For example, in the heater example (see Fig. 1) the transition from mode q_{off} to q_{on} is enabled for the temperature interval $[18; 20.1]$. Therefore, the procedure MIN-CONTROL-SIGNAL might need to consider multiple trajectories while simulating the system behavior up to the time horizon of T time units. In more details, a decision on whether to stay in the current mode or take a transition has to be made for every sampled time moment during the simulation process where a guard is enabled. This observation leads to an exponential number of induced simulations in the worst case. In order to mitigate this problem and restrict the number of considered simulations, we suggest the notion of an *important point*.

Definition 2. *A state reachable along a simulation is* important *if the mode invariant is violated or guard becomes either enabled or disabled exactly at time moment this state has been reached.*

We illustrate the notion of important points on the automaton from Fig. 1. In particular, the simulation starting in the mode q_{off} at the temperature 21° will lead to two important points when the temperature reaches 20.1° (transition from q_{off} to q_{on} becomes enabled) and 18° (invariant of q_{off} gets violated). Therefore, by restricting simulations to important points only, we can drastically restrict our search space.

These ideas are formally summarized in Algorithm 2. The algorithm has two loops. The outer loop iterates over discretized (sampled) version of the input

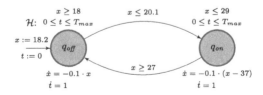

Fig. 1. Hybrid automaton for a heater [3].

set $\mathcal{U}$. Based on the chosen control input, the algorithm numerically integrates differential equations and looks up whether a reached state is important. For every important point, we add its *successor* states along enabled transitions to the set S of important points. Note that, if multiple transitions are enabled, we add *multiple* points in one step, i.e. all successor states along enabled transitions. In this way, we make sure to extend the RRT with nodes featuring new discrete modes for every discovered important point. At the same time, we always add the last simulation point to the set S to ensure it is not empty, even in case no important points have been discovered along the considered trajectory.

Procedure MIN-CONTROL-SIGNAL(x_{rand}, x_{near})
$S \leftarrow \emptyset$;
$q = \text{MODE}(x_{near})$;
$x = \text{CONT}(x_{near})$;
for $u \in \text{DISCRETIZE}(\mathcal{U})$ **do**
  $\quad t = 0$;
  $\quad$ **while** $t \leq T$ **do**
  $\qquad x = \text{ODE-SOLVER}(q, x, \delta, u)$;
  $\qquad$ **if** x *is important* **then**
  $\qquad\quad | \quad S = S \cup (u, \text{SUCC}(x))$;
  $\qquad$ **end**
  $\qquad t = t + \delta$;
  $\quad$ **end**
  $\quad S = S \cup (u, x)$;
end
return u_{min} from $(u_{min}, x_{min}) = argmin_{u, x \in S} \ \rho(x, x_{near})$;

Algorithm 2: A version of the procedure MIN-CONTROL-SIGNAL which accounts for possible non-determinism in discrete switches. The function DISCRETIZE returns a discretized version of the input set $\mathcal{U}$. The functions MODE and CONT return the discrete and continuous parts of a state, respectively. ODE-SOLVER numerically integrates differential equations for provided mode, initial state, time step and control input. SUCC returns successor states reachable along enabled transitions. The set S stores tuples (u, x) of important points and corresponding control inputs.

5   Experimental Results

Our implementation uses an input format similar to the Pysim hybrid automaton simulator built in to Hyst [3]. This allows models to be created in SpaceEx [12] and then converted and used within our RRT tool with minimal manual modification. We evaluate our algorithms on the heater benchmark [3] and the navigation benchmark [11].

Navigation Benchmark. This benchmark describes the motion of an object on a 2D plane with differential equations of the form: $x' = v_x, \ y' = v_y, \mathbf{v} = (v_x, v_y), \mathbf{v}' = A(\mathbf{v} - \mathbf{v_d}) + \mathbf{u}$ where

$$A = \begin{bmatrix} -1.2 & -0.8 \\ -0.8 & -1.2 \end{bmatrix}$$

and $\mathbf{u} = (u_1, u_2)$ is the set of control inputs which perturb the differential equations and v_d is a target velocity constant, defined individually for every discrete mode. The control inputs are constrained by $u_1, u_2 \in [-0.1, 0.1]$. We ran our algorithms for a total of 10000 iterations on the 5×5 navigation benchmark instance. Figure 2a contains a generated RRT for this benchmark instance.

Heater Benchmark. The hybrid automaton for the heater benchmark is shown in Fig. 1. Again, we ran our algorithm for 10000 iterations, which resulted in Fig. 2b.

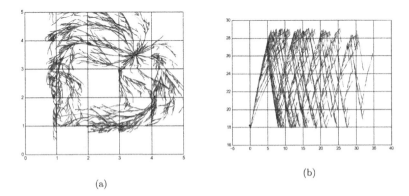

(a)   (b)

Fig. 2. (a) RRT generated for a 5×5 instance of the navigation benchmark; (b) RRT for the heater benchmark. We use different colors to illustrate the tree growth in every iteration. (Color figure online)

For both the considered benchmark classes, we observe a rather uniform state space coverage, which confirms the validity of our implementation.

6   Conclusion

In this paper, we have described our experiences with RRTs for hybrid automata. In order to account for possible non-determinism due to discrete mode switches, we have introduced the notion of important points, which intuitively captures time moments where a mode invariant becomes invalid or transitions become enabled/disabled. The evaluation shows that our algorithms lead to a reasonable state space coverage.

Acknowledgment. This work was partly supported by the Austrian Science Fund (FWF) under grants S11402-N23 (RiSE/SHiNE) and Z211-N23 (Wittgenstein Award) and by the ARC project DP140104219 "Robust AI Planning for Hybrid Systems".

References

1. Alur, R., Courcoubetis, C., Halbwachs, N., Henzinger, T.A., Ho, P.-H., Nicollin, X., Olivero, A., Sifakis, J., Yovine, S.: The algorithmic analysis of hybrid systems. Theoret. Comput. Sci. **138**(1), 3–34 (1995)
2. Bak, S., Bogomolov, S., Henzinger, T.A., Johnson, T.T., Prakash, P.: Scalable static hybridization methods for analysis of nonlinear systems. In: 19th International Conference on Hybrid Systems: Computation and Control (HSCC 2016), pp. 155–164. ACM (2016)
3. Bak, S., Bogomolov, S., Johnson, T.T.: HyST: a source transformation and translation tool for hybrid automaton models. In: 18th International Conference on Hybrid Systems: Computation and Control, Seattle, Washington. ACM, April 2015
4. Bhatia, A., Frazzoli, E.: Incremental search methods for reachability analysis of continuous and hybrid systems. In: Alur, R., Pappas, G.J. (eds.) HSCC 2004. LNCS, vol. 2993, pp. 142–156. Springer, Heidelberg (2004). doi:10.1007/978-3-540-24743-2_10
5. Bogomolov, S., Frehse, G., Grosu, R., Ladan, H., Podelski, A., Wehrle, M.: A box-based distance between regions for guiding the reachability analysis of SpaceEx. In: Madhusudan, P., Seshia, S.A. (eds.) CAV 2012. LNCS, vol. 7358, pp. 479–494. Springer, Heidelberg (2012). doi:10.1007/978-3-642-31424-7_35
6. Bogomolov, S., Greitschus, M., Jensen, P.G., Larsen, K.G., Mikucionis, M., Strump, T., Tripakis, S.: Co-simulation of hybrid systems with SpaceEx and Uppaal. In: 11th International Modelica Conference (Modelica 2015), Linköping Electronic Conference Proceedings, pp. 159–169. Linköping University Electronic Press, Linköpings universitet (2015)
7. Bogomolov, S., Mitrohin, C., Podelski, A.: Composing reachability analyses of hybrid systems for safety and stability. In: Bouajjani, A., Chin, W.-N. (eds.) ATVA 2010. LNCS, vol. 6252, pp. 67–81. Springer, Heidelberg (2010). doi:10.1007/978-3-642-15643-4_7
8. Cheng, P., LaValle, S.M.: Resolution complete rapidly-exploring random trees. In: ICRA, pp. 267–272. IEEE (2002)
9. Dang, T., Nahhal, T.: Randomized simulation of hybrid systems for circuit validation. Technical report (2006)
10. Esposito, J.M., Kim, J., Kumar, V.: Adaptive RRTs for validating hybrid robotic control systems. In: Erdmann, M., Overmars, M., Hsu, D., van der Stappen, F. (eds.) Algorithmic Foundations of Robotics VI, pp. 107–121. Springer, Heidelberg (2005). doi:10.1007/10991541_9
11. Fehnker, A., Ivančić, F.: Benchmarks for hybrid systems verification. In: Alur, R., Pappas, G.J. (eds.) HSCC 2004. LNCS, vol. 2993, pp. 326–341. Springer, Heidelberg (2004). doi:10.1007/978-3-540-24743-2_22
12. Frehse, G., et al.: SpaceEx: scalable verification of hybrid systems. In: Gopalakrishnan, G., Qadeer, S. (eds.) CAV 2011. LNCS, vol. 6806, pp. 379–395. Springer, Heidelberg (2011). doi:10.1007/978-3-642-22110-1_30
13. Lavalle, S.M.: Rapidly-exploring random trees: a new tool for path planning. Technical report (1998)
14. Plaku, E., Kavraki, L., Vardi, M.: Hybrid systems: from verification to falsification by combining motion planning and discrete search. Formal Methods Syst. Des. **34**, 157–182 (2009)

Rigorous Reachability Analysis and Domain Decomposition of Taylor Models

Martin Berz$^{(\boxtimes)}$ and Kyoko Makino

Michigan State University, East Lansing, MI 48824, USA
{berz,makino}@msu.edu
http://bt.pa.msu.edu

Abstract. We present mathematically rigorous computational methods for the transport of large domains through ODEs with the goal of making rigorous statements about their long term evolution. Of particular interest are determination of locations of attractors, reachability of certain sets, and proof of non-reachability of others. The methods are based on Taylor model verified integrators for the propagation of large domains, and heavily rely on automatic domain decomposition for accuracy. We illustrate the behavior and performance of these methods using several commonly studied dynamical systems.

Keywords: Taylor model · Verified ODE integration · Domain decomposition · Reachability analysis · Incidence matrix

1 Introduction

Taylor model methods are rigorous computational tools that allow for the representation of functional dependencies via a floating point Taylor polynomial as well as rigorous bound of the accuracy of this representation over a given domain – see [1,2] and references therein. Through the use of a naturally available antiderivation ∂_i^{-1} discussed in [2], it is possible to generate verified integrators for ODEs. In the single step, it can make use of a remarkably simple approach of rigorous enclosure of solutions of flows of ODEs, i.e. their dependence on initial condition and time, by porting the common Picard iteration scheme to the space of Taylor models [3]. Using several possible schemes for multi-steps, it is possible to achieve a far-reaching suppression of the wrapping effect (see for example [4–8] and many references therein) even in its manifestation in the remainder bound [9], which in itself is many orders of magnitude smaller than the main region covered by the flow.

Taylor model methods naturally allow for a domain decomposition approach in integration in a very similar way as it is used in many interval tools for global optimization (for a limited cross section of the many relevant books and papers, see [10–24] and references therein). In the case of optimization, the decision on whether or not to subdivide the region currently being studied, often referred

© Springer International Publishing AG 2017
A. Abate and S. Boldo (Eds.): NSV 2017, LNCS 10381, pp. 90–97, 2017.
DOI: 10.1007/978-3-319-63501-9_7

to as the box, is made based on whether the box can be excluded because its known lower bound exceeds an already known upper bound for the minimizer. If such an exclusion is not possible, the box is subdivided and each part is studied further.

On the other hand, in the case of verified integration, an excellent measure of whether a box is to be rejected is whether the remainder bound of the end result is unacceptably large, or whether the verified integrator tripped its internal failure tests for self inclusion in the integration process [3].

In the following, we will use this approach to determine the so-called incidence matrix, or alternatively a computational graph, for the flow of an ODE over a sufficiently large time domain, which can then be used for the analysis of asymptotic behavior of the solution.

2   Incidence Matrices, Graphs, and Reachability

We begin by splitting the domain of interest into n subsets covering the space, and numbering them as D_i. In practice they may consist of a collection of adjacent equally spaced boxes. We then define the so-called incidence matrix M associated with the splitting via

$$M_{i,j} = \begin{cases} 0 \text{ if it can be shown that } F(D_i) \cap D_j = \emptyset \\ 1 \text{ else} \end{cases} \tag{1}$$

where F is the flow of the ODE for the time step of interest.

So a value of 0 means that it is possible to show rigorously that an intersection does not exist. But note that in computational settings, the value 1 does not necessarily mean that there truly is an intersection, but rather it means that an intersection cannot be ruled out. The matrix can visually also be represented as a graph, where nodes denote the D_i, and vertices represent a value of 1 in the incidence matrix.

In practice it is very important that the matrix is usually rather sparse, and as the number of regions D_i is increased and the size of the D_i becomes smaller, the number of nonzero entries per D_i does usually not grow very much. This allows setting up rather large numbers of regions in the many millions, while the number of nonzero entries are only a moderate multiple of the number of entries. There is a significant body of literature related to the study of such graphs and the recovery of dynamics from it, for example [25–27] and references therein.

In the following we generate a simplified, domain decomposition based method for the determination of such a graph. For efficiency it is very important to not attempt to perform a verified integration for each of the D_i. Rather, we utilize a domain decomposing verified Taylor model integrator to first treat the entire region of interest covering all D_i, which results in a cover of the original domain space with a number of boxes that is much more manageable than the number of boxes D_i. In the next step, we identify all domain decomposed boxes in the initial domain that overlap with D_i. Then we compute a sharp enclosure for the true range of $f(D_i)$ by merely using a Horner scheme evaluation of the

Taylor model for the small domain of D_i that is actually in the range of domain of the region of interest.

In the following we will provide various examples which clarify and illustrate the practical behavior of the method.

3   The Duffing Equation

As a first example, we consider the commonly studied Duffing equation

$$\ddot{x} + \delta\dot{x} + \alpha x + \beta x^3 = \gamma \cdot \cos(\omega t), \tag{2}$$

which models a damped and driven oscillator. The goal is the integration of large initial condition set for the Duffing equation of the form

$$\frac{dx}{dt} = y, \quad \frac{dy}{dt} = x - \delta \cdot y - x^3 + \gamma \cdot \cos t, \tag{3}$$

i.e. with the parameters

$$\delta = 0.25 \quad \text{and} \quad \gamma = 0.3. \tag{4}$$

The original domain box is

$$(x_i, y_i) \in ([-2, 2], [-2, 2]). \tag{5}$$

We show the case of integrating the Duffing equation from time $t = 0$ to $t = \pi$. The given initial condition set was initially equally divided into 12×12 pieces for purpose of better visibility of the action of the flow. Many initial condition subsets completed the entire time integration without any decomposition, and only those initial condition subsets located at the place where the strong nonlinearity exists during the requested integration exhibit decomposition. Since the Duffing equation is known to exhibit chaotic motion, very rich local dynamics results, as can be seen in Fig. 1, which shows the images of the resulting Taylor model solutions with decomposed Taylor model objects at $t = \pi$ (left), and the corresponding splits in the initial condition set (right). At the final time $t = \pi$, we count altogether 343 Taylor model objects. The increase of the number of Taylor model objects is graphed in Fig. 3, starting from $12 \times 12 = 144$ initially prepared objects.

We note that the Taylor models being used are of order 33 in time as well as in initial conditions. The CPU time on a midsize notebook computer is about 21 min, and 199 domain splits happened, resulting in a final number of 343 boxes. The smallest dimension of any of the resulting initial condition boxes has an edge length of $1/(3 \times 16)$.

For better illustration, a portion of the initial condition range consisting of $3 \times 3 = 9$ divided boxes and covering the region of $[-1, 0] \times [-1, 0]$, i.e. a piece located towards the lower left from the center $(0, 0)$, is shown in Fig. 2. For this

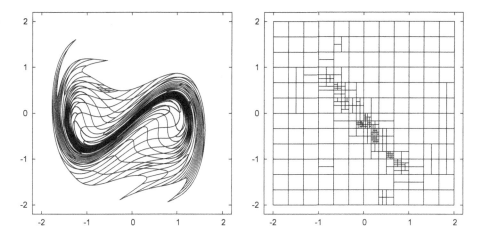

Fig. 1. Flow integration of the Duffing equation for the parameters show in the text. The right shows the original domain of interest, and the resulting subdivision of the domain in boxes that can successfully be transported. The left shows the images of the boxes under the flow. Note that the remainder error of the integration is below printer resolution and not visible in the examples.

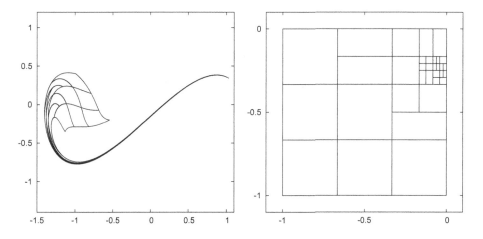

Fig. 2. A subset of the mapping of the original domain in a complicated region with much fine structure, showing that the automatic domain decomposition follows the computational local complexity of the flow.

portion of initial condition range, 24 splits happened, resulting in $9 + 24 = 33$ objects. The smallest division of the initial condition range size of $1/(3 \times 16)$ is easily observable in the x direction near the origin $(0,0)$.

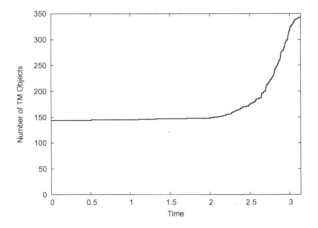

Fig. 3. Growth of the number of domain boxes as a function of integration time.

4   The Lorenz Equations

The next example discusses the Lorenz equations, which describe a simplified model of unpredictable turbulent flows in fluid dynamics. It is another frequently used example exhibiting sensitive dependence on initial conditions and chaoticity and has the form

$$\frac{dx}{dt} = \sigma(y - x), \quad \frac{dy}{dt} = x(\rho - z) - y, \quad \frac{dz}{dt} = xy - \beta z. \tag{6}$$

The standard parameter values are

$$\sigma = 10, \quad \beta = \frac{8}{3}, \quad \rho = 28, \tag{7}$$

and ρ is often varied. The fixed points are

$$(0,0,0), \quad (\pm\sqrt{\beta(\rho - 1)}, \pm\sqrt{\beta(\rho - 1)}, \rho - 1). \tag{8}$$

Rigorous flow integrations of large ranges of initial conditions have been computed using a Taylor model based ODE integrator.

In our example, we attempt a flow integration of the standard Lorenz equations for an area of initial condition

$$(x_i, y_i, z_i) \in ([-40, 40], [-50, 50], [-25, 75]), \tag{9}$$

which covers the entire region of interest for dynamics. In practice, this box of initial conditions is determined by heuristics so that an attractor is safely included inside.

The initial condition range box is pre-divided to $4 \times 5 \times 5 = 100$ smaller boxes to preserve a certain grid structure to guide the eye; so each of the original domain boxes have the size $20 \times 20 \times 20$. The integration is conducted using the Taylor model computation order 21 in both time and initial conditions until $t = 0.1$. In the process, domain splitting happened 168 times, resulting in 268 objects. The minimum size experienced in the process is an initial condition box with edge width 5, 10, 10, respectively. The computation took 27 min including miscellaneous output for purposes of monitoring, the result, and files for plotting. Figure 4 shows a grid view of the result. The z axis is shown vertically upward, and at the bottom edges, the x axis is towards the right, and the y axis is towards the left.

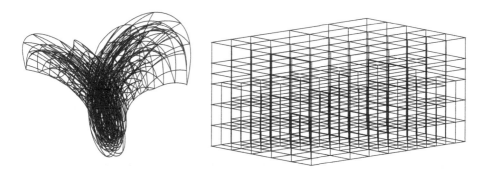

Fig. 4. Integration of the region of interest for the Lorenz system. Shown are the original domain of interest and the resulting subdivision of the domain in boxes that can successfully be transported at right, and the images of the boxes under the flow at left. Note that the remainder error of the integration is below printer resolution and not visible in the examples.

5   Conclusion

We have shown how it is possible to use Taylor model based self-verified integrators, when combined with automatic domain decomposition techniques usually used in global optimization, to obtain rigorous enclosures for flows of differential equations in an efficient manner. The resulting flow enclosures can be used to form incidence matrices of high fineness limited only by the size of the remainder bound of the Taylor models. Examples illustrating aspects of the method are given for two commonly used dynamical systems.

References

1. Makino, K.: Rigorous analysis of nonlinear motion in particle accelerators. Ph.D. thesis, Michigan State University, East Lansing, Michigan, USA (1998). Also MSUCL-1093
2. Mackino, K., Berz, M.: Verified computations using Taylor models and their applications. In: Abate, A., Boldo, S. (eds.) NSV 2017. LNCS, vol. 10381, pp. 3–13. Springer, Heidelberg (2017)

3. Makino, K., Berz, M.: Suppression of the wrapping effect by Taylor model-based verified integrators: the single step. Int. J. Pure Appl. Math. **36**(2), 175–197 (2006)
4. Lohner, R.J.: On the ubiquity of the wrapping effect in the computation of error bounds. In: Kulisch, U., Lohner, R., Facius, A. (eds.) Perspectives on Enclosure Methods, pp. 201–217. Springer, Heidelberg (2001). doi:10.1007/978-3-7091-6282-8_12
5. Stewart, N.F.: A heuristic to reduce the wrapping effect in the numerical solution of ODEs. BIT **11**, 328–337 (1971)
6. Barbarosie, C.: Reducing the wrapping effect. Computing **54**, 347–357 (1995)
7. Kühn, W.: Rigorously computed orbits of dynamical systems without the wrapping effect. Computing **61**, 47–67 (1998)
8. Nedialkov, N.S., Jackson, K.R.: A new perspective on the wrapping effect in interval methods for IVPs for ODEs. In: Proceedings of SCAN 2000. Kluwer (2001)
9. Makino, K., Berz, M.: Suppression of the wrapping effect by Taylor model-based verified integrators: long-term stabilization by preconditioning. Int. J. Differ. Equ. Appl. **10**(4), 353–384 (2005)
10. Hansen, E.R.: Global optimization using interval analysis - the multidimensional case. Numer. Math. **34**, 247–270 (1980)
11. Rokne, J., Ratschek, H.: New Computer Methods for Global Optimization. Ellis Horwood Limited, Chichester (1988)
12. Jansson, C.: A global optimization method using interval arithmetic. In: IMACS Annals of Computing and Applied Mathematics (1992)
13. Jansson, C.: A global optimization method using interval arithmetic. In: Computer Arithmetic and Scientific Computation, Proceedings of the SCAN 91, Amsterdam. Elsevier, North-Holland (1992)
14. Ratschek, H., Rokne, J.: Interval tools for global optimization. Comput. Math. Applic. **21**(6/7), 41–50 (1991)
15. Hansen, E.: Global Optimization using Interval Analysis. Marcel Dekker, New York (1992)
16. Kearfott, R.B.: An interval branch and bound algorithm for bound constrained optimization. J. Glob. Optim. **2**, 259–280 (1992)
17. Moore, R., Hansen, E., Leclerc, A.: Rigorous methods for global optimization. In: Recent Advances in Global Optimization (Princeton, NJ, 1991). Princeton Series Computer Science, pp. 321–342. Princeton University Press, Princeton (1992)
18. Wolfe, M.A.: On global optimization in R using interval arithmetic. Optim. Methods Softw. **3**, 61–76 (1994)
19. Wolfe, M.A.: An interval algorithm for bound constrained global optimization. Optim. Methods Softw. **6**, 145–159 (1995)
20. Hansen, E., Walster, G.W.: Global Optimization using Interval Analysis. Marcel Dekker, New York (2003)
21. Makino, K., Berz, M.: Verified global optimization with Taylor model methods. Int. J. Comput. Res. **12**(2), 245–252 (2003)
22. Makino, K., Berz, M.: Range bounding for global optimization with Taylor models. Trans. Comput. **4**(11), 1611–1618 (2005)
23. Berz, M., Makino, K., Kim, Y.-K.: Long-term stability of the Tevatron by validated global optimization. Nucl. Instrum. Methods **558**, 1–10 (2006)
24. Armellin, R., Di Lizia, P., Makino, K., Berz, M.: Rigorous global optimization of impulsive planet-to-planet transfers in the patched-conics approximation. Eng. Optim. **44**, 133–155 (2012)
25. Conley, C.: Isolated Invariant Sets and the Morse Index. American Mathematical Society, Providence (1978)

26. Bush, J., Gameiro, M., Harker, S., Kokubu, H., Mischaikow, K.: Combinatorial-topological framework for the analysis of global dynamics. Chaos **22**, 047508 (2012)
27. Arai, Z., Kalies, W., Kokubu, H., Mischaikow, K., Oka, H., Pilarczyk, P.: A database schema for the analysis of global dynamics of multiparameter systems. J. Appl. Dyn. Syst. **8**(3), 757–789 (2009)

A Study of Model-Order Reduction Techniques for Verification

Yi Chou$^{(\boxtimes)}$, Xin Chen, and Sriram Sankaranarayanan

University of Colorado, Boulder, CO, USA
{yi.chou,xinchen,srirams}@colorado.edu

Abstract. As formal verification techniques for cyber-physical systems encounter large plant models, techniques for simplifying these models into smaller approximate models are gaining increasing popularity. Model-order reduction techniques take large ordinary differential equation models and simplify them to yield models that are potentially much smaller in size. These approaches typically discover a suitable projection of the state space into a smaller subspace, such that by projecting the dynamics in this subspace, an accurate approximation can be obtained for a given initial set and time horizon of interest. In this paper, we present a study of model-order reduction techniques for verification with non-rigorous error bounds. We design experiments based on the proper orthogonal decomposition technique for finding reduced order models. We find that reduced order models are particularly effective and precise whenever a suitable reduced order model can be found in the first place. We attempt to characterize these models and provide future directions for reduced order modeling.

1 Introduction

In this paper, we study the potential application of model order reduction to reachability analysis of nonlinear systems. Even though significant progress has been made for linear systems [3,10], the number of state variables remains a significant limitations for applications to nonlinear systems. In this context, model order reduction techniques that approximate a large system by a reduced order system over a smaller state space have been promising [12,22]. Studies on using model order reduction of the verification of linear systems have been carried out recently [22]. Here, we report on a systematic study of model order reduction for nonlinear systems.

Our study implements a popular model order reduction approach called *proper orthogonal decomposition* (POD), that reduces a large model using a singular value decomposition (SVD) of a snapshot matrix constructed from states obtained through numerical simulations [5,18]. The SVD yields a projection from the original state space to a reduced state space over which we define reduced order ODE model. This model is often promised to be much smaller (eg. 3 state variables) when the original model is much larger (eg. 500 state variables). Hence, we study the applicability of model-order reduction techniques for reachability

© Springer International Publishing AG 2017
A. Abate and S. Boldo (Eds.): NSV 2017, LNCS 10381, pp. 98–113, 2017.
DOI: 10.1007/978-3-319-63501-9_8

computation. More precisely, we try to reduce the size of a large-scale system and then prove its safety by reachability computation, that is to prove that the overapproximation set has no intersection with the unsafe set. However, doing so forces us to work with a lower dimensional approximation, whose behaviors are empirically seen to be *close to* the original system. Therefore, the approach loses formal guarantees wrt the original model. Nevertheless, these approximations can be justified provided the error can be systematically estimated and it is understood that the original model itself is an approximation of a more complex "physical reality".

We perform an experimental evaluation using the Flow* tool to compute reachable sets over a finite time horizon using the original model (wherever possible) and the reduced order models. We compare the flowpipes so obtained against safety properties that are checked on both models. Next, we examine the effect of varying initial set sizes and time horizons for both models. We summarize the major findings of our experimental evaluation as follows:

1. Model order reduction approaches are not universally applicable. In fact, whether or not they will yield a significant reduction in the size of the model depends on how the singular values obtained during POD decay. On some systems, a rapid exponential decay yields significant reductions. However, such decays are not seen in other systems where model order reduction simply fails to yield a significant reduction or the reduced model is no easier to verify than the original.
2. Whenever a significant reduction is possible, we observe that using careful choice of the reduced model size, we obtain promising small models that are also very close to the original system. This shows that model order reduction can be considered a good approach to perform reachability analysis of large models that are otherwise out of the reach of existing approaches.
3. The performance varies, depending on the sizes of the initial sets and time horizon of interest, and also depending on the sensitivity of the original model to these parameters.

1.1   Related Work

Model order reduction (MOR) obtains a lower-dimensional approximation of a given system such that the trajectories of the approximate system are as close as possible to the original system over a set of initial conditions and time horizon. As a result, MOR is potentially a useful approach to solve control synthesis and verification problems [11,16]. A variety of approaches for MOR for linear systems exist, such as balanced truncation (BT) [16] and Krylov Methods (KMs) [20]. For nonlinear systems, the most common MOR approaches include Proper Orthogonal Decomposition (POD) and Trajectory Piecewise Linearization (TPWL). POD method calculates the singular value decomposition of *snapshot matrix* generated from trajectories sampled at certain time instants [18]. On the other hand, TPWL transforms the original nonlinear system into a combination of a set of reduced-order linear models by a process of hybridization around specific trajectory states [19]. The POD approach is used as a basis for this work, and will be described further in Sect. 3.

MOR has been explored for solving linear system verification problems [12, 13,22]. Han and Krogh developed a reachability approximation procedure with the balanced truncation reduction method, and they analyzed the error bound derived from reducing order for verification of high-dimensional linear systems [12]. They noticed that large error bounds can be avoided for initial conditions that are close to the equilibrium points of these systems. Han and Krogh extend this subsequently to consider Krylov Methods for analyzing reachability problems of large-scale affine systems [13]. Recently Tran et al. extend this work by comparing several methods for estimating error bounds in several high-dimensional linear system benchmarks [22].

However, for nonlinear systems, it is hard to estimate a conservative error bound for the reduced order model analytically. This forces us to rely in this paper on statistical techniques that do not guarantee an error bound. These techniques are justified if we can empirically show that the MOR approach approximates the model to a reasonable degree of accuracy. Since the model is often itself an approximation of the underlying physical reality, an accurate low dimensional approximation is justified. To this end, we also check if the reduced order model can preserve properties when compared to the original model.

2   Preliminaries

In the paper, we use $\mathbb{R}$ to denote the set of real numbers. Given a set of ordered variables $x_1, \ldots, x_n$, we collectively denote them by a column vector $\boldsymbol{x}$. For a column vector $\boldsymbol{x}$, its ith component is denoted by x_i. Given a variable x, we use $\dot{x}$ to denote its time derivative dx/dt.

A (nonlinear) system is defined by an ODE $\dot{\boldsymbol{x}} = f(\boldsymbol{x})$, wherein $\boldsymbol{x}$ represents the n state variables. The function f is assumed to be at least *locally Lipschitz continuous*, and therefore there is a unique solution in an open neighborhood of a given initial state $\boldsymbol{x}(0) \in \mathbb{R}^n$ for the ODE. A *state* of the system at time t, is denoted by the vector $\boldsymbol{x}(t)$.

Since most nonlinear ODEs do not have solutions expressed in a closed form, we focus instead on computing approximations of their solutions. Given an ODE $\dot{\boldsymbol{x}} = f(\boldsymbol{x})$ along with an initial condition $\boldsymbol{x}(0) \in X_0$. The exact solution is denoted by $\boldsymbol{x}(t) = \varphi_f(\boldsymbol{x}_0, t)$. This can either be numerically approximated using numerical integration approaches, or an overapproximate reachable set can be computed using numerous tools, such as SpaceEx for linear ODEs [10] and Flow* for nonlinear ODEs [7].

Flowpipe construction techniques compute reachable set overapproximation segments over a bounded time horizon. That is, each segment contains the exact reachable states over a small time interval which is also called a time step (see [1,2,4,6,9,17]). These methods are usually based on a flowpipe construction framework, that is, a reachable set segment (flowpipe) is computed based on the previous one.

3   Proper Orthogonal Decomposition

In this section, we describe the process of computing a reduced order model. We mainly focus on the method called *Proper Orthogonal Decomposition (POD)* [5, 18, 21], which projects a large-scale system to a much smaller one using a linear mapping. The linear projection is computed using singular value decomposition (SVD). The approach is also called *Principal Component Analysis (PCA)* in other areas [15].

Let $\dot{x} = f(x)$ be an autonomous nonlinear system. Furthermore, let X_0 be an initial region of interest and $t \in [0, t_f]$ be a fixed time horizon over which the system is to be approximated. The POD approach computes a matrix $n \times k$ projection matrix U_r where $k \ll n$, such that the new state variables are given by $z := U_r^T x$. Further, we require the columns of U_r to be orthonormal: $U_r^T U_r = I$. Although U_r is not invertible, we write $\tilde{x} := U_r z$ as the "representative" state for a given reduced state z. Therefore, we translate the dynamics as

$$\dot{z} = U_r^T \dot{x} = U_r^T f(x) \simeq U_r^T f(U_r z).$$

The matrix U_r is discovered as follows:

1. Randomly select an initial value $x_0 \in X_0$ and numerically simulate the time trajectory to obtain a *snapshot matrix* X using a step size $\delta > 0$:

$$X : [x(0), x(\delta), \ldots, x(N\delta)] \text{ wherein } N\delta = t_f$$

   The columns of the snapshot matrix are the states of the system at times $0, \delta, \ldots, N\delta$ for a chosen time step δ. X is thus a matrix with n rows and N columns.

2. Use singular value decomposition (SVD) to factor X as

$$X = UDV^T, \text{ wherein } U \in \mathbb{R}^{n \times n}, \ D \in \mathbb{R}^{n \times n}, V \in \mathbb{R}^{N \times n}.$$

   SVD guarantees that $UU^T = I$ and $V^T V = I$. Furthermore, D is a diagonal matrix of the singular values of X. Let the singular values be $\sigma_1 \geq \sigma_2 \geq \cdots \geq \sigma_n$.

3. Choose a number k and the corresponding k largest singular values $\sigma_1 \geq \cdots \geq \sigma_k$. The choice of this k dictates the approximation error, and is discussed subsequently.

4. The projection matrix U_r is given by the k columns of U corresponding to the chosen singular values.

Lemma 1. U_r *is the* $n \times k$ *matrix that is the minimizer of the error function:*

$$\min_{P \in \mathbb{R}^{n \times k}} \|X - PP^T X\|$$

wherein $\|\cdot\|$ *denotes the Frobenius norm. Furthermore, choosing* $P = U_r$ *provides the optimal value* $\sum_{i=k+1}^{n} \sigma_i^2$ *equal to the sum of the squares of the truncated singular values.*

One of the main assumptions that govern the applicability of this approach is that the singular values of the snapshot matrix "decay" rapidly so that

$$\sigma_{i+1}, \ldots, \sigma_n \simeq 0.$$

As a result retaining $k \ll n$ singular values is sufficient for approximating the system to a high degree, and with very low error. Note however, that if the singular values do not decay in this manner, the approach can fail to yield a sufficiently precise and small reduced order model.

3.1   An Illustrative Example

As a simple example, consider the following 3 state nonlinear system modeling three coupled oscillators. The dynamics are given as

$$\frac{d\boldsymbol{x}}{dt} = \begin{bmatrix} -2 & 1 & 0 \\ 1 & -2 & 1 \\ 0 & 1 & -2 \end{bmatrix} \boldsymbol{x} - \begin{bmatrix} x_1^2 \\ x_2^2 \\ x_3^2 \end{bmatrix} + Bu, \text{ and } x(0) = \begin{bmatrix} 0 \\ 0 \\ 0 \end{bmatrix} \tag{1}$$

where $B = [1,0,0]^T$, and input u is set to the constant 1. We simulate the system within time horizon $[0,2]$ to construct the snapshot matrix X, using step size $\delta = 0.1$. By solving the SVD for X, we obtain three left singular vectors $U_1 = [-0.9253 \ -0.3606 \ -0.1171]^T$, $U_2 = [0.3706 \ -0.7948 \ -0.4805]^T$, and $U_3 = [0.0802 \ -0.4881 \ 0.8691]^T$, with the corresponding singular values $\sigma = [5.9670 \ 0.5495 \ 0.0508]$. Thus, U_1 dominates the system's behavior, which allows to project the system into a 1-dimension subspace. With the projection $U_r^T = U_1^T$, the reduced order ODE equation becomes

$$\dot{z} = U_r^T f(U_r z) + U_r^T Bu \tag{2}$$

$$= 0.8408z^2 - 1.2482z - 0.9253u, \tag{3}$$

$$\text{with } z(0) = U_r^T \boldsymbol{x}(0) \tag{4}$$

After simulating the trajectories of the reduced model, the approximated trajectory can be obtained by projecting back to the full-order space with the relation $\boldsymbol{x}_r = U_r z$. Figure 1, shows the simulations for the original model vs the reduced order model for the state variable $x_1(t)$.

However, the situation considered for verification is complicated by the choice of a random $\boldsymbol{x}_0 \in X_0$. Ideally, by obtaining a good approximation for a single state $\boldsymbol{x}_0$, we expect that the reduced order model continues to serve as a good approximation for states that are "near" $\boldsymbol{x}_0$. Nevertheless, there are no guarantees that this is the case in practice. Therefore, we now focus on the choice of the cutoff k to guarantee an empirical error estimate over X_0 and $[0, t_f]$.

3.2   Error Estimation and Control

As mentioned earlier, the choice of k dictates the size vs accuracy tradeoff for the reduced order model. Typically, one can select the value k such that $\frac{\sum_{i=k+1}^n \sigma_i^2}{\sum_{i=1}^n \sigma_i^2} < \kappa$

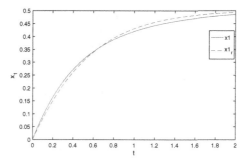

Fig. 1. Comparing the time evolution of x_1 of the original system against the approximation x_{1r} obtained from the reduced order model.

for a user-specified tolerance κ (often set as 0.01 [18]). However, the proper tolerance κ varies with different systems and furthermore, since the snapshot is constructed for one initial state x_0, the singular values σ_i do not necessarily predict the behavior for other initial states. Therefore, we measure a simulation error metric by sampling a fixed number K of states from the initial region X_0 and comparing the reduced order model with the original model:

$$e_s = \max \left\{ \frac{\|x_s - U_r U_r^T x_s\|}{\max\{1, \|x_s\|\}} \ \middle| \ x_s \text{ is a simulation sample} \right\}$$

wherein a simulation sample means a state in a (discrete) simulation trace.

Then, we choose a value of k to satisfy that the maximum error of the sampling states is smaller than simulation tolerance 0.05 in our study. If no such value can be obtained, the process of simulation is said to fail.

In order to take the size of an initial set into account in MOR, we consider to bloat the unsafe set in a reduced state space by adding a statistical error bound which is described in [14]. Although the error bound is not rigorous, it still reflects the quality of reduction.

4   Experiments

We implemented the ideas presented so far to compute a reduced order model for a given system of ODEs. In our implementation, the time horizon $[0, t_f]$, range of initial values for each variable $[x_{0,min}, x_{0,max}]$, the number of random initial simulation points l, and time step δ used in snapshot matrix are given as parameters.

Using the POD algorithm introduced previously, we have a k-order reduced model based on a projector U_r, which has a simulation error below a specified tolerance ($\delta_s = 0.05$). Next, the initial condition Z_0 for the reduced subsystem is obtained by computing $U_r^t X_0$ and then overapproximating it using a box: $[z_{0min}, z_{0max}]$. Furthermore, safety properties are bloated using the error bound $|\delta_s|$, the transformed unsafe region is also over-approximated. We use the tool

Flow* to construct the flowpipe for the reduced order model and compare this with the flowpipe for the original model whenever we are able to compute these.

In this section, we investigate the reachability of unsafe specification in several nonlinear systems with the verification technique introduced early, and further their computation will be evaluated. We first describe the benchmarks used wherein the method was successful, the reduced models for these benchmarks and flowpipes computed using the Flow* tool.

4.1   Description of Benchmarks and Results

We first present a description of some of the benchmarks and the results obtained for each benchmark.

Analog Circuits. The first circuit example is a nonlinear transmission line circuit model considered in Ref. [8], and the ODE is written as $\frac{dx}{dt} = f(x) + Bu$, wherein

$$
f(x) = \begin{bmatrix} -2 & 1 & & & \\ 1 & -2 & 1 & & \\ & \ddots & \ddots & \ddots & \\ & & 1 & -2 & 1 \\ & & & 1 & -1 \end{bmatrix} x + \begin{bmatrix} 2 - e^{0.1x_1} - e^{0.1(x_1-x_2)} \\ e^{0.1(x_1-x_2)} - e^{0.1(x_2-x_3)} \\ \vdots \\ e^{0.1(x_{n-2}-x_{n-1})} - e^{0.1(x_{n-1}-x_n)} \\ e^{0.1(x_{n-1}-x_n)} - 1 \end{bmatrix}, \quad (5)
$$

$B = [1, 0, \cdots, 0]^T$, and input $u = 0.5$ is current source entering node. The state vector $x = [x_1, x_2, \cdots, x_n]^T$ models the voltages at n points in the transmission line. For simplicity, we set all the resistors and capacitors as unit resistance and capacitance. Here, we only consider the output variable as x_1, the voltage at the first node.

Here, we consider $n = 100$, and POD reduced method can greatly decrease its dimension to $k = 2$. The initial region is

$$X_0 : \{x \mid x_i \in [0, 0.0025] \text{ for } i = 1, \ldots, 20 \text{ and } x_i = 0 \text{ for } i = 21, \ldots, 100\}$$

and the time horizon $t_f = 3$. The simulations of the original and reduced order systems are shown in Fig. 2 in solid and the dotted lines, respectively. The simulations are shown both in the original state space x and the reduced order state space z obtained by projection.

Furthermore, we compute the flowpipe segments using the Flow* tool, and the result is shown in Fig. 3. Figure 3(a) represents the flowpipe computed for the reduced order variable z_1 which contain the simulation trajectory in Fig. 2(b), and in Fig. 3(b) we further compare it with the flowpipe of the original system, also computed using Flow*. Note that in order to project the flowpipe from a low-dimensional subspace to a high-dimensional space, we choose roughly 10^4 samples of z from the flowpipe and apply the matrix U_r to project them back so that the high dimensional flowpipe can be visualized.

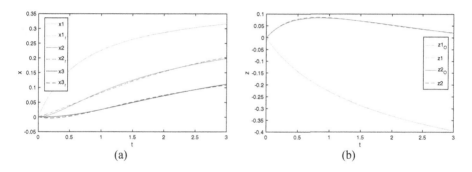

Fig. 2. A nonlinear transmission line circuit model: (a) Simulation trajectories of the original system and the reduced system in full-dimensional space. (b) Simulation trajectories of the original system and the reduced system in reduced-dimensional subspace

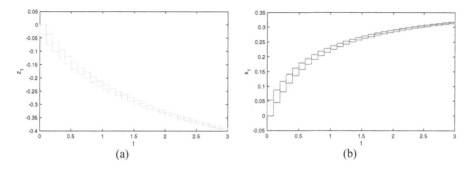

Fig. 3. Flowpipes for the nonlinear transmission line circuit model: (a) reduced model in the reduced state space, (b) comparison between the reduced model and the original model in the original state space.

The original set of unsafe states are defined as $X_f(S_n) = \{x \mid x_1 > 0.35\}$. This is relaxed to the region $X_f(S_n) = \{x \mid x_1 > 0.29\}$, taking into account a statistical error bound $|\delta_s| = 0.06$. It is further transformed to the property

$$X_f(S_k) = \{z \mid U_r(1,1)z_1 + U_r(1,2)z_2 > 0.29\}$$

over the reduced subspace. From Table 1, this safety property is not satisfied in the reduced model, whereas it is satisfied in the original model.

Next, we modify the transmission line circuit model with a quadratic nonlinearity by adding a nonlinear resistor to the ground at each node, and thus the RHS of the ODE now becomes [19]:

$$f(x) = \begin{bmatrix} -2 & 1 & & & \\ 1 & -2 & 1 & & \\ & \ddots & \ddots & \ddots & \\ & & 1 & -2 & 1 \\ & & & 1 & -2 \end{bmatrix} x - \begin{bmatrix} x_1^2 \\ x_2^2 \\ \vdots \\ x_{n-1}^2 \\ x_n^2 \end{bmatrix}, \tag{6}$$

where $B = [1, 0, \cdots, 0]^T$, input $u = 1$, $n = 100$, the initial region

$$X_0 = \{x \mid x_i \in [0, 0.0025] \text{ for } i = 1, \ldots, 20 \text{ and } x_i = 0 \text{ for } i = 21, \ldots, 100\}$$

and time horizon $t_f = 3$. In this example, POD method can reduce the dimension to $k = 2$. Figure 2 shows the simulation trajectories, and Fig. 5 shows the flowpipes (Fig. 4).

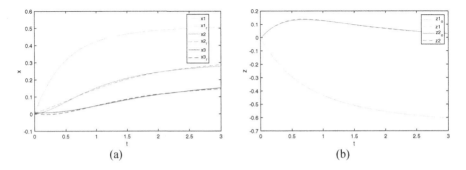

(a)   (b)

Fig. 4. A nonlinear transmission line circuit model with quadratic nonlinearity: (a) Simulation trajectories of the original system and the reduced system in full-dimensional space. (b) Simulation trajectories of the original system and the reduced system in reduced-dimensional subspace.

4.2 Fluid Dynamics

In this benchmark, we explore a fluid dynamics model for shock movement in a fluid obtained by discretizing a 1-dimensional Burgers PDE model:

$$\frac{\partial U(x,t)}{\partial t} + \frac{\partial F(U(x,t))}{\partial x} = G(x), \quad \text{with } U(x,0) = 1, \ U(0,t) = u(t), \tag{7}$$

We assume that $x \in [0, l]$, where l is the length of the modeled region, U is a conserved quantity (eg. density, heat), $F(U) = 0.5U^2$, $G(x) = 0.02\exp(0.02x)$, and $u(t)$ is the incoming flow. After discretizing the partial differential equation with $\bar{U} = [U_1, U_2, ..., U_n]^T$, where U_i approximates U at point $x_i = i\Delta x$ ($\Delta x = \frac{l}{n}$, where n is the number of grid points), we have an n-dimensional ODE equation shown below [19]:

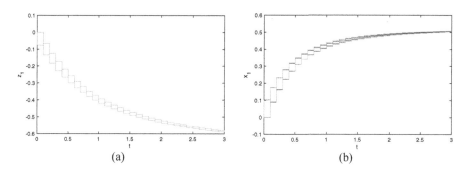

Fig. 5. Flowpipes for the quadratic nonlinearity model: (a) reduced model in the reduced state space, (b) comparison between the reduced model and the original model in the original state space.

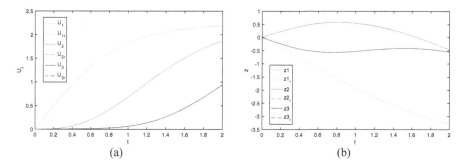

Fig. 6. Fluid dynamic model: (a) Simulation trajectories of the original system and the reduced system in full-dimensional space. (b) Simulation trajectories of the original system and the reduced system in reduced-dimensional subspace.

$$\frac{d\bar{U}}{dt} = f(\bar{U}) + Bu, \tag{8}$$

$$f(\bar{U}) = \frac{1}{\triangle x} \begin{bmatrix} -0.5U_1^2 & & & \\ & 0.5(U_1^2 - U_2^2) & & \\ & & \ddots & \\ & & & 0.5(U_{n-1}^2 - U_n^2) \end{bmatrix} + \begin{bmatrix} e^{0.02x_1} \\ e^{0.02x_2} \\ \vdots \\ e^{0.02x_n} \end{bmatrix} \tag{9}$$

where $B = [1/(2\triangle x)0\cdots0]$, and $u = 5$ in our study. Also, we consider the initial region

$$\bar{U}_0 = \{\bar{U} \,|\, U_i \in [0, 0.0025] \text{ for } i = 1, \ldots, 20 \text{ and } U_i = 0 \text{ for } i = 21, \ldots, 100\}$$

and $t_f = 2$. In this case, the dimension is reduced considerably from $n = 100$ to $k = 3$. Simulating the trajectories, there is no noticable difference between that from full-order model and that from reduced-order model, which is shown in Fig. 6. As we expected, Fig. 7 compares the flowpipes for the reduced model contain that of the original model.

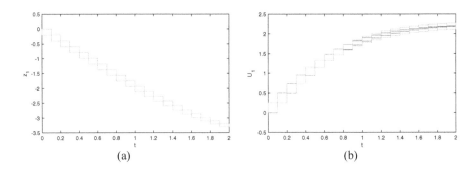

Fig. 7. Flowpipes for the fluid dynamic model: (a) reduced model in the reduced state space, (b) comparison between the reduced model and the original model in the original state space.

Table 1. Checking properties for the original model S_n vs. the reduced order model S_k: for each benchmark, the initial condition region and time region are described in the text.

Benchmark	$X_f(S_n)$	Safe	$X_f(S_k)$	Safe
Analog circuits.1$(n = 100)$	$x_1 \geq 0.35$	Yes	$U_r(1,1) * z_1 + U_r(1,2) * z_2 \geq 0.29$	No
	$x_2 \geq 0.25$	Yes	$U_r(2,1) * z_1 + U_r(2,2) * z_2 \geq 0.19$	No
	$x_3 \geq 0.20$	Yes	$U_r(3,1) * z_1 + U_r(3,2) * z_2 \geq 0.14$	Yes
Analog circuits.2$(n = 100)$	$x_1 \geq 0.6$	Yes	$U_r(1,1) * z_1 + U_r(1,2) * z_2 \geq 0.54$	Yes
	$x_2 \geq 0.4$	Yes	$U_r(2,1) * z_1 + U_r(2,2) * z_2 \geq 0.34$	Yes
	$x_3 \geq 0.2$	Yes	$U_r(3,1) * z_1 + U_r(3,2) * z_2 \geq 0.14$	No
Fluid dynamics$(n = 100)$	$x_1 \geq 2.5$	Yes	$U_r(1,1) * z_1 + U_r(1,2) * z_2 +$ $U_r(1,3) * z_3 \geq 2.426$	Yes
	$x_2 \geq 2$	Yes	$U_r(2,1) * z_1 + U_r(2,2) * z_2 +$ $U_r(2,3) * z_3 \geq 1.926$	Yes
	$x_3 \geq 1.5$	Yes	$U_r(3,1) * z_1 + U_r(3,2) * z_2 +$ $U_r(3,3) * z_3 \geq 1.426$	Yes

4.3   Evaluation

We now discuss the results over the benchmarks in detail. Table 2 presents the details of the benchmarks, the sizes of the reduced order model, the running time for flowpipe computation in the original vs reduced models, and the error bounds for each of the benchmarks used in our example. As expected, we have nonlinear systems as large as 500 variables over which we obtain very small reduced order models that are handled by Flow* whereas the original system cannot be within the given time out for one hour. However, for the P53 model, we observe that Flow* is able to compute the flowpipe for the original model but times out on the reduced order model. There are many reasons: for one the number of state variables is just one indicator for the difficulty of a flowpipe construction problems. Factors that depend on the behavior of the model's time trajectories also play a critical role.

Figure 8 plots the singular values for the fluid dynamic and the P53 models. In one case, we note the rapid exponential decay in the singular values allowing us to achieve a large reduction, whereas in the other we see that the singular values remain relatively large in magnitude.

Table 2. The computation time and the statistical error bound corresponding to different benchmarks: n is the dimension of a original system, S_n is the reachable set for the original system, $T(S_n)$ is the time in seconds for flowpipe over the original system, k is the dimension of a reduced-order abstraction, S_k is the reachable set for the reduced system, $T(S_k)$ is time taken by flowpipe computation on the reduced model, $|\delta_s|$ is the total statistical error bound, OOT represents "out of time" with the time limit $= 1\,\mathrm{h}$.

Benchmark	$T(S_n)$	k	$|\delta_s|$	$T(S_k)$
Analog circuits.1($n = 100$)	59	2	0.06	1.5
Analog circuits.1($n = 500$)	OOT	2	0.13	1.8
Analog circuits.2($n = 100$)	498	2	0.06	0.5
Analog circuits.2($n = 500$)	OOT	2	0.13	0.5
Fluid dynamics($n = 100$)	205	3	0.074	1.4
Fluid dynamics($n = 500$)	OOT	3	0.23	2
Cellular P53 regulation($n = 6$)	110	4	51	OOT

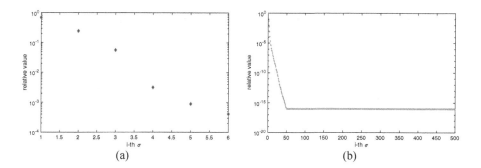

(a)   (b)

Fig. 8. The singular values obtained for (a) Cellular P53 regulation benchmark. (b) Fluid dynamics benchmark.

Next, we vary the sizes of the initial region for each of the benchmark while continuing to look for a reduced model that conforms to a fixed error bound. Table 3 shows the results. Here, we note that as the initial region is made larger, the time taken to estimate the error bound increases, the size of the model increases and so does the computation time for the flowpipes. In some cases, the model order reduction is no longer successful in obtaining a flowpipe within

Table 3. Varying initial region for benchmarks. Initial set region is $X_0 : (x_1 \in [0,b], \ldots, x_{20} \in [0,b], x_{21} = 0, \ldots, x_n = 0)$ for varying values b. n is the dimension of a original system, k is the dimension of a reduced-order model, $|\delta_s|$ is the total statistical error bound, OOT represents "out of time" with the time limit $= 600\,\text{s}$, $T(S_n)$: flowpipe computation time for original model, $T(S_k)$: flowpipe computation on reduced order model, T_M: time taken for model order reduction, $T(\delta_s)$ time taken for error estimation and calculation of k.

Benchmark	b	$T(S_n)$	k	$|\delta_s|$	$T(S_k)$	T_M	$T(\delta_s)$
Analog circuits.1	0.0025	59	2	0.06	6	1	5
($n = 100$)	0.01	63	2	0.24	7	2	5
$t_f = 3$	0.05	65	3	1.13	23	3	5
	0.1	67	15	2.1	OOT	1.5	5
Analog circuits.1	0.0025	OOT	2	0.13	6	2.2	46
($n = 500$)	0.01	OOT	2	0.5	7	1.5	60
$t_f = 3$	0.05	OOT	3	2.5	24	2	45
	0.1	OOT	16	5	OOT	2.7	45
Analog circuits.2	0.0025	136	2	0.06	0.5	3	39
($n = 100$)	0.01	140	2	0.24	0.5	3	46
$t_f = 3$	0.05	140	5	1.1	23	3	39
	0.1	142	16	2.1	OOT	3.6	42
Analog circuits.2	0.0025	OOT	2	0.13	0.5	6.4	374
($n = 500$)	0.01	OOT	2	0.5	0.6	7	375
$t_f = 3$	0.05	OOT	5	2.5	23	9	434
	0.1	OOT	17	5	OOT	7	418
Fluid dynamics	0.0025	66	3	0.074	1.4	3	18
($n = 100$)	0.01	73	3	0.22	1.5	3	18
$t_f = 2$	0.05	72	5	0.98	14.8	3	18
	0.1	83	18	2.0	OOT	3	18
Fluid dynamics	0.0025	OOT	3	2.3	1.6	9	271
($n = 500$)	0.01	OOT	3	2.5	1.5	8.7	294
$t_f = 2$	0.05	OOT	10	2.5	OOT	8.1	272
	0.1	OOT	17	4.99	OOT	10	277

the time limit of 600 s for these benchmarks. The loss of effectiveness of MOR when the initial set is large, while not unexpected, is a limiting factor for its application to verification problems. Table 4 shows the results. Here, we note that the sensitivity to changes in initial conditions and time horizon is highly model dependent. Nevertheless, we notice a clear trend that as the time horizon is increased, the reduced order models are generally larger and harder to compute with.

Table 4. Varying time horizon t_f for the benchmarks with a fixed parameter $b = 0.01$ of the initial condition region. See Table 3 for the legend.

Benchmark	t_f	$T(S_n)$	k	$|\delta_s|$	$T(S_k)$	T_M	$T(\delta_s)$
Analog circuits.1	1	20	2	0.24	2	0.5	1.5
($n = 100$)	3	63	2	0.24	7	1.7	5
	6	213	2	0.24	15	3	9
	12	263	2	0.24	33	5	19
	20	416	3	0.24	160	8.5	27
Analog circuits.1	1	OOT	2	0.52	2	1.9	27
($n = 500$)	3	OOT	2	0.52	7	1.5	60
	6	OOT	2	0.52	15	3.1	94
	12	OOT	2	0.52	33	4.3	165
	20	OOT	3	0.52	100	6.3	308
Analog circuits.2	1	47	2	0.24	0.3	1	12
($n = 100$)	3	140	2	0.24	0.5	3	46
	6	268	2	0.24	1	5.8	90
	12	502	2	0.24	2	13	175
	20	OOT	3	0.24	13	45	350
Analog circuits.2	1	OOT	2	0.5	0.3	2.5	131
($n = 500$)	3	OOT	2	0.5	0.6	7	376
	6	OOT	2	0.52	1	15	OOT
	12	OOT	2	0.52	2	26	OOT
	20	OOT	3	0.52	13	47	OOT
Fluid dynamics	1	30	2	0.22	0.3	1.5	18
($n = 100$)	2	73	3	0.22	1.5	3	18
	4	158	5	0.24	34	4.4	70
	8	325	8	0.23	OOT	5	100
Fluid dynamics	1	OOT	3	0.91	0.6	4.7	143
($n = 500$)	2	OOT	3	2.5	1.5	8.7	249
	4	OOT	5	0.59	34	16.8	563
	8	OOT	8	0.52	OOT	35	OOT

5 Conclusion

In conclusion, we have studied the effectiveness of model order reduction methods for nonlinear systems. We note that the approach is promising whenever the singular values show a rapid decay, failing which it does not produce significant reductions. We also note that the reduced order models provide for highly effective verification and are accurate enough for many tasks. Thus, MOR seems effective in a class of systems obtained by discretization of PDEs provided we are interested in a small set of system variables. Furthermore, MOR becomes more challenging as the initial conditions and time horizon of interest become larger.

References

1. Althoff, M., Stursberg, O., Buss, M.: Reachability analysis of nonlinear systems with uncertain parameters using conservative linearization. In: Proceedings of CDC 2008, pp. 4042–4048. IEEE (2008)
2. Asarin, E., Dang, T., Girard, A.: Hybridization methods for the analysis of non-linear systems. Acta Inf. **43**(7), 451–476 (2007)
3. Bak, S., Duggirala, P.S.: Hylaa: A tool for computing simulation-equivalent reachability for linear systems. In: HSCC, pp. 173–178. ACM (2017)
4. Berz, M., Makino, K.: Verified integration of ODEs and flows using differential algebraic methods on high-order Taylor models. Reliable Comput. **4**, 361–369 (1998)
5. Chatterjee, A.: An introduction to the proper orthogonal decomposition. Curr. Sci. **78**(7), 808–817 (2000)
6. Chen, X., Ábrahám, E., Sankaranarayanan, S.: Taylor model flowpipe construction for non-linear hybrid systems. In: Proceedings of RTSS 2012, pp. 183–192. IEEE Computer Society (2012)
7. Chen, X., Ábrahám, E., Sankaranarayanan, S.: Flow*: an analyzer for non-linear hybrid systems. In: Sharygina, N., Veith, H. (eds.) CAV 2013. LNCS, vol. 8044, pp. 258–263. Springer, Heidelberg (2013). doi:10.1007/978-3-642-39799-8_18
8. Chen, Y., White, J., Macromodeling, T.: A quadratic method for nonlinear model order reduction, pp. 477–480 (2000)
9. Chutinan, A., Krogh, B.H.: Computing polyhedral approximations to flow pipes for dynamic systems. In: Proceedings of CDC 1998, vol. 2, pp. 2089–2094 (1998)
10. Frehse, G., et al.: SpaceEx: scalable verification of hybrid systems. In: Gopalakrishnan, G., Qadeer, S. (eds.) CAV 2011. LNCS, vol. 6806, pp. 379–395. Springer, Heidelberg (2011). doi:10.1007/978-3-642-22110-1_30
11. Gugercin, S., Antoulas, A.C.: A survey of model reduction by balanced truncation and some new results. Int. J. Control **77**(8), 748–766 (2004)
12. Han, Z., Krogh, B.: Reachability analysis of hybrid control systems using reduced-order models. In: Proceedings of the 2004 American Control Conference, vol. 2, pp. 1183–1189, June 2004
13. Han, Z., Krogh, B.H.: Reachability analysis of large-scale affine systems using low-dimensional polytopes. In: Hespanha, J.P., Tiwari, A. (eds.) HSCC 2006. LNCS, vol. 3927, pp. 287–301. Springer, Heidelberg (2006). doi:10.1007/11730637_23
14. Homescu, C., Petzold, L.R., Serban, R.: Error estimation for reduced-order models of dynamical systems. SIAM J. Numer. Anal. **43**, 2005 (2005)
15. Jolliffe, I.T.: Principal Component Analysis, 2nd edn. Springer, Heidelberg (2002). doi:10.1007/b98835
16. Lall, S., Marsden, J.E.: A subspace approach to balanced truncation for model reduction of nonlinear control systems. Int. J. Robust Nonlinear Control **12**, 519–535 (2002)
17. Nedialkov, N.S., Jackson, K.R., Corliss, G.F.: Validated solutions of initial value problems for ordinary differential equations. Appl. Math. Comput. **105**(1), 21–68 (1999)

18. Pinnau, R.: Model reduction via proper orthogonal decomposition. In: Schilders, W.H.A., van der Vorst, H.A., Rommes, J. (eds.) Model Order Reduction: Theory, Research Aspects and Applications, pp. 95–109. Springer, Heidelberg (2008). doi:10.1007/978-3-540-78841-6_5
19. Rewieski, M., White, J.: Model order reduction for nonlinear dynamical systems based on trajectory piecewise-linear approximations. Linear Algebra Appl. **415**(2), 426–454 (2006)
20. Salimbahrami, B., Lohmann, B.: Order reduction of large scale second-order systems using Krylov subspace methods. Linear Algebra Appl. **415**(2), 385–405 (2006)
21. Stadlmayr, D., Witteveen, W., Steiner, W.: Reduction of physical and constraint degrees-of-freedom of redundant formulated multibody systems. J. Comput. Nonlinear Dyn. **11**, 031010–031010-9 (2015)
22. Tran, H.D., Nguyen, L.V., Xiang, W., Johnson, T.T.: Order-reduction abstractions for safety verification of high-dimensional linear systems. Discrete Event Dyn. Syst. **27**(2), 1–19 (2017)

Author Index

Printed in the United States
By Bookmasters